Oakland Public Library
Oakland, CA 94612

To Elvis, With Love

To Elvis, With Love

by Lena Canada

Everest House
Publishers　　New York

Published simultaneously in Canada by Beaverbooks, Pickering, Ontario

Dedication

They called you a great man.

And you were. Great in a way few have ever known.

They wrote your name with capital letters and surrounded you, making you inaccessible to most people. You wore a crown of fame and glory. You dwelt in a castle of fortune and success. You were carried high on the waves of admiration and exaltation. All of us knew your talents as a performer, your magnitude as a star. But comparatively few have been as privileged as I have been, to experience in such a direct way the true measure of your greatness as a person and as a human being.

They called you a great man, and rightfully so.

It took true greatness for a man of your fame to pause to give your personal attention to the very smallest, perhaps the most insignificant, among your multitude of fans.

This is the story of one of the smallest of God's many children who was also one of your most devoted fans.

Her name was Karen.

Each day of her short life was colored with pain. But she reached longingly out of her misery toward the shining light of your stardom, and you became a joyful dream in her heart. She gave you her love. It was boundless, innocent, and pure, as only the love of a child can be.

For a long time I have wanted to tell you about the happiness you gave Karen. I have wanted so much to thank you. But great men are so difficult to reach.

And now you are dead.

Elvis, this book is for you. With admiration, with gratitude, and, most of all, with love . . .

Part One

Part One

As I lie in my bed at dawn, watching the day begin, my memories return—and I remember how everything began. . . .

The distant, monotonous traffic noise from busy boulevards plays a sad tune-without-end in my ears. The darkness, the shadows surround me, making everything diffuse and unreal. Very quietly and very slowly I say her name aloud into the darkness and listen to the silence that follows. A feeling of emptiness and bitterness grows within me. It flows like a faint shivering through my body and I no longer make any attempt to stop it. I have learned to recognize pain as it approaches me. Pain, which fills the emptiness within me with a throbbing ache.

Even here in America, I cannot fully escape it. Thousands of miles away and so many years later, there is still a small corner of my heart where pain is a permanent resident. It is like a white heat from out of the past, burning in my early morning loneliness into the pattern of my daily life.

Like mothers everywhere, out of some age-old, instinctive custom, I seek refuge and consolation by watching my children at sleep. The house is still curled up in peaceful relaxation around me, savoring its last few moments of uninterrupted rest. The whole world seems to be holding its breath in awe and reverence at the new day which is about to be born.

There is a quality of serene beauty about the two little heads on their pillows. Their faces are so peaceful. Their cuddly little bodies are flung out in such careless abandon among the covers. In only a few short hours they will be tumbling around in the backyard with the restlessness which only little boys know and can fully appreciate. Their knees will be scratched, their cheeks flushed, and their shrill voices will envelop the neighborhood with all the joyous innocence and carefree exuberance of their young lives. They are healthy, safe, protected. Their world is carefully provided with all the comforts money can buy, and they have inexhaustible supplies of a love which is limitless.

I clasp my hands in prayer, gratefully acknowledging the greatest gift I have ever received. These two, who are so healthy, so perfect, so full of life. These two who are mine.

Protected by my loneliness and hidden by the gray shadows of the early morning, I allow the tears to run freely down my cheeks as I watch them. And my mind wanders, once again, back to another time and place, a world so far and yet still so close that it seems like a dream.

I remember Karen.

I was so painfully young then, and so vulnerable. I was by no means old or mature enough to handle Karen, the little girl whom destiny so willingly placed in my charge. But I struggled with my assignment and I became her mother, her sister, her friend and guardian for the short time she stayed with me. She was the first one to ever ac-

quaint me with the apparently unjust and random allot-
ment of pain and unhappiness in the world. But she was
also the one who showed me the miracles that can be accomplished through infinite love and boundless, never-end-
ing faith.

She was frail and thin and physically crippled. Her
eyes were dark with frightened loneliness. They were filled
with pain, as though she had seen all the misery in the
world and mourned over it. She fought an eternally brave
fight to keep me out of her life and out of her heart. She
placed on my weak shoulders burdens of worry, sadness,
pain. She forced me mercilessly to stare cruelty and helplessness in the face and to shudder at my own inadequacy.
Still, the void she left behind was one which cannot be
filled, and the lesson she taught me is one I shall carry
within me forever.

In the early morning hours I cry softly for her and for
all the miseries of mankind and for the suffering that innocent children must bear.

This is Karen's story.

The Brown House stood in regal splendor in an opening
among the trees.

It was one of the largest institutions for the handicapped in Sweden. Or rather a branch of it, for the main
building—which housed the adult wards, the prosthesis
laboratory, and the out-patient clinic—was located in the
midst of the city; a busy place, humming with activity and

surrounded by smog and freeway noises. Some kind-hearted administrator had wisely decided that this was no place for children, so instead, they were sent to the rambling, two-story country house that was located in the as yet undeveloped and deserted outskirts of Stockholm. It had been carefully converted into a combination boarding school-hospital for some twenty physically handicapped children.

It was a charming, old-fashioned building, which, thanks to its size, gave an impression of majestic dignity. At the same time, the generous use of natural wood and brick gave it a warm and inviting appearance. A passerby could easily have mistaken it for a hotel or an inn, a comfortable resting spot nestled in the fresh countryside.

The Brown House sprawled in the forest, much like a friendly, old bear taking a nap in the peaceful September afternoon.

The sun poured its rich autumn gold over the world on the morning I met Karen. I remember that I felt happy as I traveled through the fresh, chilly countryside on my way to the little school for the "different." Happy, because the world was clear and golden, sparkling in ripe maturity.

The restlessness of summer had calmed in anticipation of the winter which was to come. It was like the time in your life when you are old enough to have attained some sort of understanding of life and still young enough to enjoy it.

The house was comfortably embedded in a sloping hill

side, brown, timbered and gracefully framed by black tree trunks and yellow leaves. The lawns were wide, well kept, and strangely empty. Somehow I had expected to see children there.

Happiness followed me up the curving driveway. It was my silent, invisible companion across the front yard. It was a warm, comforting feeling. I felt an abundant satisfaction just because I was walking right there at that time. Later I would remember my feeling and regard it as a happy premonition.

In front of the main entrance I hesitated for a moment, discovering that it apparently was seldom used. It still looked new, as though it did not really belong to the rest of the house, for the wheelchairs had their own sloping entrance a little further away. The wooden boards were scratched and bruised, marked by lively, careless use. There was no question about where the inhabitants of the house went in and out.

I heard distant laughter from deep within the belly of this majestic house. A twinkling melody of clear children's voices seeped through an open window somewhere. I lingered by the front steps, enjoying the taste and smell of my rich contentment. I wanted to keep that moment, remember it, as though I had known, already then, that this was something that I would not easily forget.

Once inside the deserted hallway, I hesitated, suddenly overcome by uncertainty. The floor seemed to stretch out for miles in front of me, hospital green, well scrubbed, and with just the faintest odor of disinfectant about it. Where it finally ended was a wide stairway leading upward to some distant region from where noise and laughter could be heard.

There was a table by the opposite wall with a large mirror above it. There I was—a lonely and slightly nervous figure, with worried eyes, pale complexion, and long, straight, blond hair falling down my back.

I stared at my reflection in the mirror, wondering what that naive, bewildered stranger was doing there. I was barely nineteen and just out of school. So far my encounters with life had been of a painful and confusing nature.

I had been fortunate enough to be born into a financially comfortable family. Money was the only aspect of my life that gave me no worry. My father was a navy officer who commanded his wife and children with the same cold superiority with which he presided over his submarine crews. Whenever intimidation did not quite seem to suffice, or direct orders were not obeyed quickly enough, he was given to fits of uncontrolled anger, mostly of a brutal, physical nature.

Even my earliest childhood memories are tainted with fear. I can still taste the sour feeling of anguish as I walked home from school with a report card containing something less than an *A*, knowing that I would not only be whipped and beaten, but prevented from going to bed at night and drilled and examined until I could demonstrate to my father that I had memorized my homework by heart.

I can recall the agonizing torture of watching my mother being slapped and kicked until she was an unconscious heap on the floor, and I know the helpless feeling of being too young and too powerless to intervene. Anger and hatred were with me from the earliest beginning, it seems. But they were my secret companions. So frightful was my father's reign, and so enormous the consequences of any form of rebellion, that I never dared show my hostility in the open. Instead, with fear being a tight knot in my stomach, I became a model child: studious, quiet, and polite.

Since my father feared that any form of social life might interfere with my studies, the friendships I formed were few and meager in nature. Friends were not allowed at my house, and the few times I tried to get away with something behind my father's back, the fear of being found out was always so great that it spoiled my fun anyway. The first time in my life a boy asked me to a movie, my father was waiting for me at home. When I showed up a half-hour late, holding hands with my friend, I got a beating so bad that I could not go to school for two days. Thus, from an early age, I became a loner, an introvert, and a dreamer. So powerful was my father's adverse effect on my character that these are still major components of my personality.

My mother was a shy and timid woman who had escaped her own father's domineering personality, only to find herself married to a man of even more brutal tendencies. Somewhere, deep in her heart, she must have known that things could have been different, but the mere thought of revolt or mutiny was in itself too frightening. She was a beautiful, but uneducated, country girl, very much impressed with the shiny brass buttons on my father's captain's uniform. She had moved out of her father's house and directly into her married home, and had never had an opportunity to try her independence. The prospect of standing alone in the world on her own two feet, without anybody by her side, was just too much to even consider. Besides, the social status and financial security my father had to offer were important ingredients in her life.

I formed a strong bond of deep emotional dependency with my mother and my younger brother. Together, the three of us would huddle in the locked bedroom when my father's temper approached another outburst. We were locked together in the fear we had of him, the suppressed hatred, and the carefully concealed anger. My mother, despite all her supposed adult maturity, was just as weak and just as helpless in front of my father as me and my brother. We both felt a sense of responsibility for her, and protectiveness. In spite of the age difference and the fact that she was my mother, it was almost as if she and I both knew that I was the stronger of us, and somehow this put me in charge. I can still recall being ten years old, comforting my sobbing mother and cleaning her bleeding face, all the while wishing desperately that somebody bigger and more capable would come and take care of *me*.

I loved my mother deeply, but it was the protective feeling of tenderness one has for somebody smaller and weaker. And there was a good portion of resentment mixed into my feelings. Instead of being the strong, central figure of security I needed the most, she added to the burdens my father had already put on my shoulders. Between the two of them and my younger brother, I was forced to grow up much too fast, and to assume responsibilities I was not ready for. With bitter envy, I would observe the comparatively carefree lives of my school friends, and the gap between me and the rest of the world became even greater.

At thirteen, when it was suddenly discovered that an automobile accident had caused the development of a tumor in my right arm, I was almost relieved to spend the next two years in and out of hospitals. Without complaint, I underwent operation after operation—each time losing more and more of the use of my arm and hand. Finally, a dedicated doctor in preventive medicine suggested amputation as the ultimate recourse, and before long I was transferred to an institution for the handicapped where that sort of thing was handled as a matter of routine.

Although fear was by this time an ice-cold lump in my throat, I recall being surprised at the sense of normalcy that existed at this institution. It did not take long before wheelchairs and braces became a natural and automatic part of my environment, and the initial shock of seeing human deformity subsided. I shall never forget the casual air of a young woman who had lost both of her legs in a traffic accident.

"Well, most people have two legs to carry them; some have one; and then there are a few of us who don't have any—"

For a couple of agonizing months I lived in the world of the handicapped while my case was being evaluated. The verdict was finally brought in and found to be in my favor. Just as I was beginning to quietly resign myself to the idea of having only one arm, I was once again transferred back to the hospital for more operations.

By the time I was fifteen, my parents' marriage had disintegrated to the point of disaster. My mother was beginning to honestly realize the self-destructive futility of the course she was headed for. Little by little, she had developed a supportive relationship, this time with one of the doctors who had been treating me. With his help, she was finally able to make the one and only gesture of firm resolution in her life: she stood up to my father, at last, and demanded a divorce. After a grueling court battle, my father mercifully disappeared from our lives.

The king was dead, thank God, and we celebrated his demise. The tyrant was no longer looming like a dark cloud over our lives. My brother and I were eagerly looking forward to the normal, peaceful family life we would now be able to have with our mother. We had wished for it for a long time. We had hoped and prayed, and here at last was our dream about to come true.

But what we did not realize was that our mother's helplessness was truly genuine, and that she was not emotionally strong enough to take the lead, no matter what the situation. She was one of those people who simply cannot function alone, but only as a complement to someone stronger. Without the dominance of my father, she was lost. Instinctively she must have known this, because almost immediately she set out on her search for someone to take charge of her life. Within a matter of weeks, her friendship with the doctor had turned into a romantic involvement, and she was totally and completely absorbed in her own, newfound happiness.

Sad and happy at the same time, I observed the miracle of love transform my mother into a self-centered, coquettish woman with little time left for her responsibilities to her children. Once again, I was bothered by the apparent reversal of roles and felt more strongly than ever that I was the older and more mature, whose duty it was to protect her from evil and hurt. A month or so later, when she happily announced her decision to move in with the doctor, it was with quiet resignation that I gave her my blessing and sent her on her merry way. I was, by this time, painfully aware that my mother was not, and would never be, the kind of dependable parent who stands with her feet planted firmly on the ground, stirring pots and pans and polishing silverware, always there with a warm embrace whenever you needed her.

So, at the age of fifteen I found myself reluctantly playing the role of mother subtsitute to my eleven-year-old brother. I did not particularly like the idea. I was nothing but a child myself, fresh out of the hospital, and rather than being charged with new responsibility, I wanted more than anything to be taken care of. I wanted to be little and helpless and allowed to openly admit my fears. But this was not to be for me.

Alone in an oversized apartment in a wealthy neighborhood in Stockholm, my brother and I did the best we could to take care of each other, go to school, and keep our little household together. Every so often, my mother would drop in for a brief visit to make sure we were all right, and would leave generous amounts of money in place of the time and affection she was just too busy to give. I tried desperately to be understanding, to feel genuinely happy for her, and to hide my resentment. But when the day came, about a year later, when my brother decided to go live with my mother and the doctor, I cried bitterly with frustration and loneliness. I hated everybody: my father for his horrendous brutality; my mother for her desertion; my brother for leaving me with an emptiness and loneliness greater than ever before.

Resolutely I decided that my relationship with my family was over. I knew then, that things would never again be quite the same. From that point on, whatever little connection there was between us slowly disintegrated, until my mother's phone calls came only once a month, and my handsome weekly allowance arrived by registered mail.

Thus, at nineteen, I was living by myself in a large, elegantly furnished apartment, with money available whenever I needed it, and an excess of time on my hands.

Loneliness and confusion had brought me to the Brown House. I had come looking for a job—not for the money, but for something to do with my time and with myself. I stood there in the empty hallway, staring at my own helpless reflection in the mirror, searching desperately for some purpose to my life, hoping I had come at last to a place where I could love and be loved in return.

The Brown House embraced me with friendliness.

The sun was pouring in through the tall windows. A shaft of light danced and sparkled in the air. It ran in a stream of fluid gold across the floor, as though it was purposely reaching for the large table where some children were busily occupied with paper and crayons. It was a serene, peaceful picture. Honest and truthful, yet with a touch of fairy-tale unreality. It seemed too beautiful, too perfect to be real.

These children were like a bouquet of spring flowers picked too roughly by a child's eager, impatient fingers. Some stalks were just a little too short, some petals had fallen off. A few of the leaves were torn or crumpled. They were all so fragile. You may say that these flowers were feeble and often ruined, but you could never deny the innocent beauty they still possessed. Yes, the children at the table were, in a manner of speaking, crumpled and torn like the imaginary flowers. They were delicate little plants, picked in the good Lord's vast garden. One had lost its stalk. Another was missing a petal or a leaf. But together they still formed a beautiful bouquet.

Stiff little hands groped for new colors. Rigid arms fumbled among the clean sheets of paper. A twittering little voice exclaimed that her work was finished.

"Just like any other children, anywhere," was the thought that pursued me. And yet different. Painfully different.

I felt flushed and torn with mixed emotions. These damaged children radiated life so intensely. It confused me. It was a feeling so strong and so real that I felt as if I could actually reach out and touch it. Perhaps, I came to realize later, it had to be that way. Perhaps there was no alternative but for the children in the Brown House to enjoy life in a very special way, living each moment more passionately than the average, normal child.

This was the world of the different, or at least one little corner of it. This was their school and their home, this rambling, brown house. And there I was for the first time among them. Healthy. Perfect. Confused.

The Brown House nursed a peculiar family with many children. It seemed as though the good Lord had wanted to build a friendly shelter where he could gather all of his lost little sheep. It was a refuge, a home.

The children's backgrounds were all different. They came from misery and tragedy everywhere. They were rich or poor, loved or despised, accepted or rejected. Fate selected them without regard to class or condition. But eventually they were all brought together in this huge, brown house in the secluded countryside because they were all damaged, defective, each to a different degree.

There were about twenty of them, ranging in age from approximately six to twelve. Most of them were victims of varying degrees of cerebral palsy, from the paraplegic to the only mildly afflicted. But there was also the little boy who was completely normal except for a shocking skin disease which made him look as if he were recovering from third degree burns all over his body, with itchy, flaking skin and bright red patches of flesh in between. There was another little boy, whose muscular and skeletal system was so weak that if anybody tapped him even lightly on his back he would fall into a crying, helpless pile on the floor. There was at least one bleeder, and there were several children who had had colostomies. One little girl was hydrocephalic, with a head way out of proportion to the rest of her body. One or two others had inoperable spinal tumors growing like bright red oranges on their backs. Most of them were of almost-average intelligence and only slightly retarded; one or two were perfectly normal; and perhaps four or five were so grossly retarded that they had to be considered "vegetables." There was also one boy who had been involved in a severe traffic accident, and who babbled incoherently about the time when he "used to go to a regular school," and remembered how the other kids used to tease him. Another one, who really did not belong in the Brown House, ran around on all fours dressed in a nightgown, insisting he was a dog and demanding to be fed in a bowl on the floor.

The center of most families is usually one dominant character. And even this motley group had its leader. She was the headmistress. A mild, wise woman, she was as comforting and understanding as a mother of that many children had to be, just as efficient and capable as an administrator should be. She was tall and fair, with regular, handsome features. Her angular limbs and firm hips gave her the appearance of a Nordic peasant, which reminded me of earthiness, religion, and solid, fundamental values. But there was at the same time a tender air of sensitivity about her and a great gentleness and wisdom. I liked the headmistress from the first minute I met her. To me she represented all the warm security that I so desperately had wanted from my own mother. She was strong and capable, with many years of nursing training behind her. I admired her patience and maturity long before I ever heard her tragic life story. There must have been a time when she was just as young and innocently naive as I was, before cruelty chose her to be one of its victims.

It was said that she once had a devoted husband and a lovely little son. A traffic accident took them both away from her: her husband to death's eternal darkness, and her son to life's. The little boy remained in a coma for weeks. When he finally regained consciousness, he was completely retarded. He could no longer control his bodily functions. He did not recognize his mother. There was only one solution. He became a lifetime prisoner in an institution for the mentally retarded.

Now she was a mother again. She was the headmistress of the Brown House—the strong, good-hearted headmistress whose door was always open to anybody who needed to talk, and whose compassionate smile was always shining like a warm summer sun over the children.

I was walking by the headmistress's comforting side one morning when everything quietly began. Her crisp apron rustled softly. Her voice was low and soothing. Every so often her hand would travel absentmindedly over a little head, stroke a cheek, pick up a toy. She was my interpreter, my competent guide, this very first morning of my journey through the world of the different.

"Different children," she said thoughtfully. "No, you are pronouncing it wrong. The emphasis should be on *children*. That's what they first and foremost are. Anything else is secondary and less important."

The headmistress knew her children. She loved them and suffered with them. She knew their difficulties and their endless struggle. She knew that most of the children in the Brown House were still happy, still protected, both by age and by innocence. She was well aware of the dangers that lay ahead for them, and she realized, painfully, that many of them would never have to face the problems of adulthood. Puberty was where many a handicapped child was stopped and often doomed. Those who managed to fight their way through adolescence were the ones who possessed a certain amount of strength and adaptability, not only to physical change but to mental and emotional pain as well. And they would need this strength. Many of the children in the Brown House would get lost on that road which often leads through suffering, rejection and alienation, the characteristic ingredients in the handicapped child's life. The headmistress knew this. She suffered at the thought of it, but at the same time she rejoiced in her conviction that among the children in her care there were a few who would enjoy a relatively long, comparatively useful, and possibly even happy life within the confines of an institution. Perhaps it would be just three or four, but considering the odds that were against them, that meant three or four miracles.

In the meantime she had used all her resources and all

available means to turn the Brown House into as friendly and happy a place as it could possibly be, with colorful bedspreads, well-scrubbed floors, and with the shelves in the playroom loaded to capacity with toys and books. And from the kitchen there was always the delicate aroma of freshly made coffee, enclosing the house in a warm wrap of friendliness.

There was a look of contentment on the children's faces, a feeling of harmony and peace. Somehow, it confused me, but it also took the edge off the pain I felt over seeing the physical deformities of their little bodies.

Little did I know that right there, among the chattering group in the playroom, was one whom happiness had not been able to reach.

"And this is Karen," the headmistress said. It seemed to me, for a moment, as though a shadow of worry passed over her face.

And so without warning or preparation, destiny brought me to the little girl who was to guide my life in an entirely new direction. I looked right into her dark, mournful eyes where so much was written which I would later learn to read and interpret. I did not suspect what the future would hold for me. How could I? Fate's capricious gestures are things I never bothered to try to understand.

At that moment Karen was just one small member of the large family in the Brown House. With disinterested eyes I regarded her that first time. I noticed the thin little body which looked bony and malnourished in the big wheelchair. I could easily see the outlines of the rigid muscles under the white skin on her forearms. Her hands, cramped in almost arthritic deformity, fluttered restlessly from side to side. The tendons at the side of her neck were a bundle of tense, white strings. Her legs were covered by a blanket.

She was a small child, and the spastic contractions of her skinny body made her appear grotesque and horrifying. Her face was narrow and unnaturally pale, with hollow cheeks and thin, shivering lips. Only her eyes seemed to be alive, burning somber and mournful from out of the dark circles under them with an intensity of grief and pain which I could not avoid noticing. Her hair was silky and light brown and fell carelessly down her back. She looked haunted. Yet, at the same time indifferent and distant. A strange combination. Or maybe not so strange after all.

Her eyes fluttered coolly over my face, as if she was looking for defects or imperfections. Unwillingly, I felt my smile slowly dying on my lips, freezing into a rigid, unnatural grin which it was never intended to be. Somehow I sensed that this child did not want any smile from me, no false attitude of friendliness, no polite affection. We were strangers. There was no reason for approach or contact. I was nothing but another occasional visitor walking through the room. She did not ask my errand or mission. All she wanted was that I leave her alone as soon as possible. I was an intruder from the outside, healthy world. I was looked on as having no place in the Brown House, and therefore I had to be cautious, reserved.

She regarded me with the same remote disinterest with which one looks at the passengers in a bus or a subway. Distant. Distracted. With critical reservation. Not a smile, not even the shadow of any expression passed over her face. She seemed to be very far away. Yet, at the same time I had an uncomfortable feeling that she carefully reacted to every little detail in the environment. She appeared sensitive, delicate and cautiously aware. The first encounter between Karen and me was just so: cold, suspicious, empty.

I was a foreigner, an outsider, new, unknown, probably dangerous. Karen did not like me. I knew it. I sensed it. Automatically. Instinctively. As I turned away, three words came to mind. *Noli me tangere.* Do not touch me. That was the message in her eyes.

I thought I detected an expression of pain in the headmistress's eyes as we proceeded. At the moment, I did not quite understand the reason for it, but now I know. It is painful to give love which is never accepted. I was to experience it myself.

But with a house full of children, there is no time to look worried. The frown which Karen had caused on the headmistress's face many eager little hands wanted to erase. She knew it. She let them succeed. She smiled. And we went on.

Our inspection tour ended. I sat down for a cup of coffee with the headmistress and some of the other staff members.

There they were; the speech therapist, the social worker, the physical therapist, the physician. They were people as common in a physically handicapped child's life as a gardener or a janitor is in ours. The conversation was easy and friendly, the way it becomes when people know each other well. There was a comforting atmosphere of insight and understanding surrounding the table. These people shared the same goals. They all belonged to the same, big family, fighting the same struggle. They were knit together in their work and by their love for the little children in the Brown House and handicapped children everywhere. I envied their togetherness and dedication. With a feeling of quiet comfort I suddenly knew that I would like to come back to this rambling Brown House. I wanted to belong to them too, and be part of this big, peculiar family.

Outside the window the afternoon softly turned into husky evening. The trees stood majestically tall and black, with a rustling cover of leaves at their feet. The countryside was serene and peaceful. At a distance, I could hear a voice calling the children to dinner.

Slowly, unnoticeably, the evening dusk deepened, and the day ended.

The Brown House refused to leave my mind. Resisting temptation has always seemed quite impossible to me, and sometimes even quite unnecessary. I gave in. Destiny helped me willingly.

"Why don't you come out here for a while and try this kind of work?" the headmistress had casually suggested. That was the sort of invitation I had been looking for.

A week later I was once again walking up the curved driveway that unfolded in front of me like a satin ribbon among the solid, oak trees and towering pines. The sky was dressed in misty gray and the leaves on the ground lay in soggy, brown clusters across the lawn. But the Brown House still stood in majestic splendor at the end of the road, breathing warmth and friendliness.

A feeling of comfort rushed through my veins as I saw it sitting there, so dignified, so confident, among the trees. It was almost as if I had been on a long journey and finally returned home. Everything settled in a neat, precise pattern.

The Brown House received me with a spontaneous embrace. Many eager little arms reached out for me, making room for me in the togetherness that was theirs. And without hesitation I opened my arms and heart to them. For how could I not love them?

It is fascinating to explore a new friendship. To look for all the traits and details which form a personality, to put together weaknesses and strengths, faults and assets, into one, coherent piece. To catch an expression here and a gesture there and find that they are all composite and integral components of the individual. To discover a whole person, complex, intriguing, exciting and unpredictable.

I was groping in many directions and felt many little hands reaching out for me. Making friends with children is either very difficult or very easy. With the children in the Brown House it was easy, and perhaps undeservedly so. I discovered with satisfaction that I was surrounded by new friends. Dependable. Affectionate. Eager and anxious to be liked in return.

The Brown House closed its arms around me. I

learned its rhythm and felt its pulse inside and outside myself. I was adopted by its large family. I was given a place, a role, a task, a purpose in my life.

The day started early at the Brown House.

Before seven, the children were up. The bedrooms were buzzing with activity, the water splashed in the bathrooms and little hands fumbled with night braces that had to come off and socks that needed to be put on. The elevator made trip after trip with the wheelchair children, while the wide stairway moaned quietly under crutches and heavy orthopedic shoes. By eight, they were all lined up, with shiny, clean faces and combed heads by the long tables in the dining room upstairs.

Mealtimes were always highlights of the day. The wise headmistress realized that in a schedule which, of necessity, was the same from day to day and from week to week, food had come to mean excitement for many of the children. It was one of the few variations that broke the monotonous routine. She made sure that there were frequent, unexpected, special treats. In this regard she was totally supported by the broad-hipped, soft-hearted cook, who saw food as one of the ultimate ways of expressing love for one's fellow man.

Breakfast was a time of gearing up for the day, and reaffirming friendships from the night before. There was an atmosphere of joyful anticipation around the tables, and even the most severely crippled children who needed to be fed appeared content and smiling. It was almost as though the arrival of another day in and of itself brought new hope into their lives.

By eight-thirty breakfast was over and the children were taken to their respective classrooms. The Brown House relaxed somewhat after the bustling activities of the early morning. The windows were opened wide, the bedrooms cleaned and the floors mopped before the personnel had a chance to regroup in the dining room for a well-deserved cup of coffee and some casual small-talk.

With the exception of a short break when colostomy bags were checked and those children who needed it were diapered, the rest of the morning went by peacefully. This was the time when special conferences were held and informal discussions about research and new therapy methods occurred. Every so often, the staff physician would drop in unexpectedly and, coffee cup in one hand and cigarette in the other, would give a casual update on one of the children. Inevitably, just as we got involved in the most interesting part of the discussion, the bell would ring and school was out.

After lunch, the Brown House again became feverish with excitement as everybody prepared to go outside. Sweaters had to be fetched, jackets found, wheelchair children buckled securely into their seats, and the tool shed unlocked so that everybody could have access to balls, buckets, bikes, and wagons. The ambulatory children had free run of the lawns and the front yard. The less fortunate had to take turns being wheeled around. They would sit pitifully by the side, trying desperately to take delight in the other children's enjoyment.

Karen was always one of those on the sidelines. Her chair would be safely positioned away from the line of action, the brakes secured, and for the next hour or so she would be left to herself. There was so little that could be done for this child.

With pain written in her dark eyes, she would stare at the distant treetops, dreaming wistfully of happier places and easier times.

Dinner was served early—before four o'clock—to give plenty of time for winding down and preparing for the night. The headmistress herself supervised the dining room, and frequently pitched in to help feed one of the children. She sat like any other mother in the midst of her children, pouring milk, cutting meat, and was not the least bit concerned that her starched white apron got smudged by food stains.

After dinner came quiet time in the playroom. We would read or talk. Some of the children had homework to prepare for the following day. Some wrote letters. Others, who deserved a special reward, were allowed to go downstairs to the TV room and look at cartoons until it was time for bath and bed. There was a light, evening meal, and then it was once again time for night braces, special corsets, and medication.

By seven-thirty the lights went out, and after a couple of last-minute requests for water and some hushed whispering between the beds, silence took over and the Brown House settled down for the night.

I shall never forget the children in the Brown House. In my mind they will always live. There they have names and faces, character and personality. There they all have their own, separate corner. I know that I am unfair in letting them remain gray and anonymous here. They all deserve to be mentioned. Each one of them could play the main part in a story like this. Yet, I will pass them by. I will make them diffuse and unidentified. I will keep them at a distance. I want to make room for only one—Karen.

Ironically, she was the only one who at first rejected me and regarded me with cold indifference. She was the only one who deliberately stayed beyond my reach and the only one who was not about to become my friend.

I will do it to make her part as big and beautiful as possible so that no one may compete with her for performance or applause.

I will do it, because this is her story.

Memories flash through my mind. Odd little pieces of remembrance, diffuse and incomplete, but perhaps still with a certain amount of importance.

The headmistress is walking around the room with a box of candy which she generously hands out to her many children. Red, green, yellow little balls. Sweet, sticky, delicious. Many eager little hands are pulling at her skirt. Karen is the only one who shakes her head and solemnly turns away. . . .

The sun is dancing across the playroom floor. There, in the golden light, the girls are playing with their dolls. Awkward little hands are attempting to dress, feed, and spank their naughty children. They are concerned, busy little mothers. Karen is off in a corner, watching with eyes that are dark with fearful contempt. . . .

The speech therapist comes on her regular visit. She is a sparkling, happy woman who tempts everybody to join in her cheerfulness. She sits by the piano, leading her little group in a cavalcade of playful music. Chirping voices rise and fall, each one according to his own skill and ability. Slightly dissonant. Somewhat slow. Only Karen is silent, always silent. . . .

The memories are always the same. Karen stayed outside, enclosed in her own mysterious world. So distant. So lonely. So desolate.

I was standing by the window, looking at the scattered little figures outside in the yard. The children had been taken outside on their regular midmorning break of clean, fresh air and outdoor play. There they were, some bundled up in wheelchairs, others moving around on crutches or dragging around awkwardly with their clumsy leg braces. It was pathetic. A tragic picture that somehow made me think of a prison yard. A gravel square, an hour's worth of chilly air. That was their freedom.

Karen was sitting by herself, as usual. She seemed to be miles away from the other children. Their cries and laughter bounced against her invisible, impenetrable wall. She had a dreamy look on her face. Her eyes touched the distant, naked treetops, searchingly, longingly. Every once in a while a frown would cloud across her features. Her hands opened and closed with rhythmic regularity. She was a picture of loneliness and desolation.

I heard a soft rustle behind me, and there was the headmistress. Compassion filled her eyes. She followed my gaze through the window. Anxiously, like a mother bird, she watched over her children. Finally, her eyes reached Karen and lingered there, just like mine had only a moment ago. She sighed softly, perhaps involuntarily.

"Poor girl," I said.

She nodded thoughtfully.

"Our difficult child," she said tenderly.

"What can be done?"

She shrugged.

"I wish I knew," she said. "Perhaps the only thing to do is to wait and see. Karen needs time to find herself. She is suffering from severe emotional shock you know, aside from her physical limitations. We still have not quite figured out why—"

"She seems intelligent."

"Karen is much brighter than she lets anybody know. She is too intelligent for her age actually, which may very well be part of the problem."

We remained silent for a while, pondering over life's incomprehensible injustices.

Intelligence is so overrated, I thought. We make the intellect too valuable and too important. We forget that too much intelligence is just as great a handicap as too little.

"Poor little girl," I said again.

"She is not even nine years old," the headmistress said, letting her gaze rest on me for a moment. "Come with me. Let me tell you—"

We entered her little room behind the office. I sank deep into a chair, enjoying the comfort of her presence. She was a woman who radiated a primitive, earthy motherliness which made me want to cling to her for strength and understanding, just like the wounded children in the Brown House.

I listened to Karen's story. It was a meager account, supported by a few gloomy facts. Institution life is so arranged that any trace of feeling or reason is carefully obliterated from the records and only the barest minimum of facts are allowed to remain. Dates. Names, perhaps. Occasionally addresses. I suppose that a description of all the overwhelming emotion that was experienced, all the tragedy that exists behind an institutionalized child is not just convenient or possible to keep in the record. It would clutter the case history too much, and take valuable space away from all the medical data which must be recorded.

From outside the window I could hear the children's voices and remembered Karen among them, so lonely, so abandoned.

The headmistress was playing with her bracelet. Distractedly, almost restlessly, as if she were trying to free herself of some inner worry or tension.

She explained the anguished torment that a young mother experiences when she realizes that she has given birth to a defective child. She said that the decision to cut all ties, sever all connections and allow your daughter to be raised as an orphan in an institution for the handicapped is not necessarily one of cruelty or cowardice. She also spoke with knowledge and experience about the tragedy and injustice an abandoned, handicapped child's life contains, and of the tortured loneliness that so often follows.

Karen's mother was young and hopeful. She did not have the inner strength to cope with the shock of having a severely handicapped infant. Out of what must have been panic and desperation, she made her painful decision within a matter of days after Karen's birth.

She signed the required papers and made the necessary arrangements to relinquish both duties and rights, and disappeared forever out of Karen's life.

I have spent endless hours thinking about the young woman who was Karen's mother. I can feel her hopeful expectations during nine, long months of waiting. I can picture her grief and despair over the miserable little baby that was born to her. I know her suffering, her regret, her guilt.

But I would also like to believe that the reason for her monumental decision to let Karen grow up in an institution was one of love—disappointed, tortured love, but still love. Any woman who spends nine months carrying a child within her body, who goes through the agony of the birth process itself, and then attempts to walk away and make a clean break must inevitably find herself caught in a lifelong vise of pain and regret.

How many times has she in her tortured thoughts seen Karen grow up in despair and loneliness? How many unanswered questions still haunt her?

I wish I could reach out and touch her hand for a moment of comfort. I wish I could tell her about Karen. And about Elvis—generous, compassionate Elvis Presley.

It might set her mind to rest and give her some relief from her personal agony.

Karen was sent to an institution to grow up among her own kind, those who were "different". She was classified CP—cerebral palsy.

Her medical portrait described her in horrifying detail: ". . . severe case of spastic quadriplegia. Gross contractures. Rigidity. Heavy blocking. Breathing is athetoid. Speech—defective or possibly quite retarded. Vision, hearing—good. Mental impression—excellent. . . ."

Nature had been careless in the creation of her body. Her legs would not carry her. Her arms would not obey. Her speech consisted of guttural sounds which could barely be understood. All of this could be traced back to brain damage which had occurred before or during birth itself. Nobody could with definite certainty determine where or when, and nobody could cure a brain injury of this kind.

Nevertheless, every cerebral palsied child can improve in line with his capabilities, provided the proper physical education and training is given. It is a disease which has never yet been cured, only alleviated. Karen's life was carefully and routinely sectioned off into a regular pattern of various forms of therapy: physical therapy, speech therapy, bath therapy, braces, exercises, wheelchair.

Her eternal struggle had begun.

It was an uneven fight, and unjust. It was a battle without end or termination, without pause. It was the struggle for her own body. The object of the fight was to capture something which, in a sense, she already had. She had to make progress and gain territory within the country of her own body to control a muscle, to learn a movement.

Karen's struggle had been fought by many before her. Some had had the strength to carry it on and on. Others, weaker ones, had finally given in to bitterness and despair.

A little girl does not always have the strength and patience that life demands.

Something happened within Karen. Something which I shall never be able to properly give a name. Karen herself did not know what it was, but it was threatening and choking. Perhaps her difficulties all of a sudden appeared too great. Perhaps the weakness inside her grew. Nobody can struggle forever with constant disappointment. We all have our moments of dark despair when we would like to turn our backs on the world. Who has not wished to be a clam, a snail, or an oyster, with a protective shell to hide behind?

The "different" world of the handicapped, the defective, is a busy place, a vast working-field. Everybody is too busy, too loaded down with work. Nobody has time. Everything is so urgent, so important.

Ultimately it becomes a tragic world. We forget that which is most important in all situations—the individual. A lonely, confused little girl so easily gets lost in the machinery of an institution.

The white-clothed men and women in Karen's world were always in a hurry. Their days were cramped with chores and crowded with importance. They fluttered like huge, white birds on their rounds through the wards, burning with zealous ambition to be efficient. Perhaps Karen was frightened by their hurry. Whatever was growing inside her never found an outlet, never found a response. It remained imprisoned in her heart, gradually forming bitter thoughts and gloomy conclusions. Her worried mind became bruised and scarred. Her frightened soul became as hurt and wounded as her body.

Nobody ever quite understood exactly what happened with Karen, but she turned into herself. She turned her back to the world. But she found no relief or comfort even within herself. Just an endless, black sea of hurt and confusion. Karen was constantly misunderstood, repeatedly disappointed, forever defeated.

At last she resorted to the only way that seemed to remain for her. She erected an invisible wall between herself and the rest of humanity. She locked up her little heart and threw away the key.

When the headmistress finally stopped talking, I was overcome by emotion. I do not know if I was touched by the cruelty and helplessness she described, or if it was simply any woman's instinctive pain when she sees a child suffer. Suddenly I was burning with desire to do something for Karen.

"Oh, yes," the headmistress said wearily. "We all want to help, of course. If only—"

And all of a sudden I could sense her desperation. She had done all she could without getting any closer to Karen. Others had tried, with or without professional help, and without succeeding. I had only made a couple of weak efforts so far. What made me believe that I would be able to accomplish anything where so many had failed before me?

Nevertheless, I would try. What could possibly be greater than to fight to save a human child, I thought to myself. My defeat would not be any greater than anybody else's had already been.

I told the headmistress. She gave me a gentle smile. Not aloof, not ironic, not condescending, but weary. Her eyes traveled outside the window, once again in search of Karen's thin face.

"Do whatever you can," she said, "just don't expect too much."

I promised her I would do everything I could. It would not be a one-way street. The Brown House meant a home to me. And Karen was more than just another sick, unhappy child. She was my one opportunity to have someone to love and to find at last someone to love me.

I plunged into my care of Karen with an insatiable need to be needed.

Some of the working conditions at the Brown House, which to the rest of the personnel meant inconvenience and disadvantage, were exactly the things I was looking for. The work was hard and physically tiring. It meant full-time involvement, which left little room for personal thought. This suited me very well. My confusing family arrangement bothered me very much. The initial anger I had felt was beginning to subside, and pain and loneliness, had come in its place. It hurt me to come home at night to the large, empty apartment which always looked exactly the way I had left it in the morning. The Brown House, and its busy schedule, kept me occupied until late in the evening. My work schedule was such that I had to be there before seven in the morning when the children first woke up. In the middle of the day, I would have several hours off, but the idea of spending an hour on the train home, only to turn around and come back again, was never particularly attractive. Instead, I would remain at the Brown House and spend my free time with Karen.

Shortly before dinnertime I was back on duty again for the remainder of the evening until the children were asleep. If I puttered around long enough afterwards, I could arrange to "miss" my 8:00 train and would have to wait an additional hour. That way, by the time I finally got home, it was late enough to go straight to bed and I would not have to confront my loneliness. I had it all figured out.

I was a good employee, conscientious and dedicated. I never complained about the hard work or the awkward hours, and whenever someone was out sick, I could always be called upon to put in extra time. Little did the head-mistress know that I had good reason for working so hard. My father had laid the groundwork, of course, by physically beating into my soul the values of self-discipline and dedication. Although he was no longer present in my life, I was too conditioned to try to break out of the mold he had erected. I always had the fearful feeling that if I did, he would somehow find out about it and find some way to punish me.

The "loss" of my mother and brother hurt me terribly. The infrequency of the phone calls and the strange distance whenever we did see each other were constant reminders of how little they cared. I felt like an orphan or a stepchild. It was important for me to find another context where I could fit myself in, establish some contact, and somehow prove to myself that even I had a place where I belonged.

The Brown House suited my purpose almost to perfection. As long as I worked long and hard enough, the thoughts of my mother could be pushed aside, and were not quite so acutely painful. At the same time, I was trying to become an integral and important part of the Brown House.

I made friends with some of the other young women working there and, for the first time in my life, got an opportunity to enjoy other people my own age. It seemed that the young women employed at the Brown House were of a very particular breed. Sensitivity to the needs of others, and a deep-rooted love for children with special problems were absolute requirements. A good sense of humor and basic human charity helped keep things in their proper perspective. In addition, a strong back was important for lifting wheelchairs and children in heavy braces, and a strong stomach was needed for changing diapers and colostomy bags.

It was inevitable that a strong bond developed between the women there. We shared our meals, discussed our problems, and traded free hours. On our days off, we would frequently go into town shopping together. Many evenings, exhausted, we would all steal into the kitchen for a cup of tea and end-of-the-day gossip. Alerted by the sounds, the headmistress would come into the kitchen and, after she had lightly reminded us that we were in violation of regulations, would eagerly join our group.

It was a good time. I was reaching out, making contact. The Brown House became my focal point, and its inhabitants my family. Karen was, of course, becoming the center of my universe.

What nobody ever really seemed to understand was that I needed Karen just as much as she needed me. The hard work was only a cover-up, a form of escape from bitter thoughts and tremendous loneliness. What everybody took to be unselfish dedication was nothing more than a desperate attempt to make myself important—somewhere, somehow.

In time, I was able to give my mother the same emotional detachment she gave me. The Brown House became my life, my world, my home. My apartment in the city became nothing more than a storage room for my personal effects, a place for nightly stopovers.

Karen the unhappy. Karen, the unreachable. Karen, the aloof, the cold, the distant. Her names were many, but each described a lonely, desperately alienated, helpless little girl.

I helped her put on her coat, pulling it softly and carefully over her rigid arms. I pushed her in the wheelchair on long walks through the countryside. I sat for hours by her side, reading stories, dressing dolls, painting, cutting, pasting, singing. All to no avail.

I talked. Happily and cheerfully. Softly and confidingly. Convincingly, I thought. I talked about everything and anything that happened to pass through my mind. I talked to cover up the empty distance between us. I talked to hide the accusing silence. I talked stubbornly, for ears that did not hear, to a face that did not care, until there were no words left.

I moved into her territory with awkward clumsiness and rude impertinence. I stood there with my ardent ambition, my youthful thoughtlessness and my selfish proclamation that help had arrived. There was neither pride nor tactfulness for either Karen or myself. I did not even have my strategy worked out properly, but was struggling with plans and methods all mixed into one, great confusion. I was desperate. I was young, anxious, enthusiastic. There was no time to waste. I was in a hurry to help Karen. I was determined to find her, save her, and love her. I was perhaps, even cruel.

Certainly I must have been ridiculous.

Yet Karen stayed behind her invisible wall. She crawled even further into her corner in an anguished attempt to escape my impertinent persistence. Her face became even more pale and serious. Her eyes pleaded that she wished to be saved from my noisy intrusion into her life. She shut her ears to my voice. She fluttered away like a wounded bird.

"Karen, look here! Did you ever try to make the soap float in the bathtub? Look! Oh no, it's sinking—"

"Hey Karen, let's go out and explore the world, shall we? Just the two of us. Which way would you like to go today? Shall we go and see if there is still ice on the lake? Are you warm enough—"

"Guess what I have got for you! Look, a whole box full of that striped candy that I know you like. Go ahead, taste it! Come on, now. Just one? Please—"

"Guess what happened this morning—?"

"Shall we read this book or would you rather listen to Winnie the Pooh?"

"Can you make a picture of a porcupine? Look here! It's very easy, really—"

Questions without answers, endlessly, hopelessly . . . .

Words. Words. Words to search for that which was never found. To fight but never win.

I searched. I fought. I struggled while my enthusiasm was rich and my ambition abundant. I still searched and fought long after they had become worn and threadbare. Karen remained as distant as a daydream.

I had tried to build our relationship with words. I had been talking in an attempt to narrow the deep crevice that separated us, to budge the distance, fill the emptiness. But talking has its limits, like everything else. Finally there comes a point where you run out of words. I sensed that I was wasting my time. One morning my words died in the middle of a sentence. Suddenly I heard how empty and false they sounded.

I grew quiet, filled with a feeling of overwhelming futility.

Karen did not even seem to notice. She did not care whether I was talking or not. She sat like before, huddling in her wheelchair, a slight frown between her eyebrows. In-accessible. Remote. Her eyes regarded me as coldly as if we had never met, as if I were a stranger. And perhaps after everything, that was all I was.

Silence took over.

It was a pitiful, destructive silence. It was the silence of defeat. It was the kind of silence that follows when there is nothing more to say. It grew like a prison wall around us, cold, suffocating, like death itself.

The days were getting shorter and darker. Fall had already passed its sultry, colorful maturity.

What weird mission was it that I had undertaken to carry through? What kind of strange bird was Karen, anyway? An injured little bird. So what! Aren't we all injured little birds, more or less? I wanted so much to be mild, good, and understanding. I wanted to come into her life soft and pure, like a saint or an angel to rescue her from pain and loneliness. I wanted to reach out and bring her in touch with the warm togetherness of the rest of the family in the Brown House. But Karen would not let me.

Who was this child who obviously found it so easy to be cold and unfeeling? Could she not see my pitiful struggle? My ardent longing to help? How could she so stubbornly refuse me even the slightest hint of encouragement? Did she not understand that I felt pain, too? Just one little sign. That was what I was asking. Just one small indication that what I was trying to do was right and good. Was I really so badly mistaken? It certainly seemed so.

The tears burned in my throat. "You wait!" I thought furiously. "Just you wait, Karen! I will show you that my stubbornness is greater than yours. The day is going to come when you will have to understand—"

Perhaps that was what she was really waiting for? Somebody with the strength and power to outlast her. Somebody who would not give in, no matter how long or how merciless the journey seemed. Someone who cared enough not to be defeated by her invisible wall but who would break it down and bring her out into the open.

Her indifference was beginning to hurt me. It was no longer just a challenge, but was starting to feel like a weapon she was using against me, to ward me off and to keep me away. My cheery hopefulness was gone. I felt self-ishly that I was entitled to some recognition and deserved some encouragement for still stubbornly being in the game.

I wanted to slap her, shake her, get some life into her.

But you do not slap an injured little bird. You cup your hands carefully around it. You give it warmth and protection. You give it time. You want, hoping that it will survive, and wish that someday it will fly from your hands on strong, powerful wings.

Most of all I wanted her to let me love her and to show that she knew I was alive, that I existed.

Each afternoon, just before dinner, came that horrible hour that was set aside for exercise. This was the time when Karen reluctantly was taken from her wheelchair and lifted onto the large foam-rubber mattress in a corner of the play-room.

Nobody paid much attention. The children in the Brown House were well acquainted with all forms of ther-apy. To them, it was as natural a function as eating or sleeping. They all took their turn at various times of the day. Nobody too eagerly, of course. To these children, exer-cise was not a means of making a beautiful body slimmer or already bulging muscles even stronger. Exercise meant hard work, and precious playtime sacrificed. Karen hated it perhaps just a little bit more than the rest of them.

There she was—vulnerable and exposed in all her ugly deformity. There was no longer any blanket to hide the skinny sticks that were her legs, or the feet that fell so limp and listless inwards. Her arms were cramped in an awkward, defensive pose up around her neck—almost as if she were trying to hide her face from the world. Her eyes grew large with fear and pain, pleading silently to be put back in the comforting embrace of the wheelchair. She looked like a frazzled little bird with two broken wings, wanting nothing more than to be returned to its nest to die in peace. I always felt sorry for her, and had to remind myself that what we were about to do was both necessary and important.

At first, her muscles were slowly and carefully massaged, to bring the blood circulating to all parts of her body. Then her feet were gently rotated and her legs stretched and bent as far as they would allow—and then just a fraction of an inch more. Karen winced in pain. I would look at the bony limb in my hands and wince in pain, too.

We would work our way upwards. The physical therapist had shown me how to raise Karen into a sitting position and keep her there, for a moment, before she tumbled back down again. Then came the arms—the stiff, reluctant, fragile arms—the clenched hands, and the rigid fingers.

It was called "exercise" but I was the one getting a workout: pulling, stretching, twisting, and manipulating. Karen suffered through it all, just biding her time until it would all be over.

Once a week, she was exercised in the pool in the swim hall. This was not quite so painful or strenuous, since the water seemed to have a limbering effect on her muscles and the whole concept of gravity changed. Firmly hooked up to a floating device, Karen tried to reach for various objects in the water. Thoughtfully, I would sit by the side of the pool and watch Karen almost gracefully catch the rubber ball the physical therapist was tossing to her. I think we were all just as delighted to see the feats she could perform in the pool.

She enjoyed the water, the warm, buoyant feel of it against her body. I could tell by the way she gingerly moved her arms, surprised to find that she could control them. Her features relaxed. The deep frown between her eyebrows disappeared. Once or twice I could have sworn that a smile flashed across her eyes. Only for an instant, and I could never be quite sure, but the look on her face reminded me of the way she looked when I would wheel her through the forest: as if she had just been released after a lifetime in prison.

But there was always that moment when she was lifted out of the pool and put back into the wheelchair. Her limbs quickly resumed their old hostility, her fingers became disobedient, and the frown found its old place between her eyebrows. We had to wait another six days to test the miraculous water again. There would be six more sessions on the rubber mat in the playroom. Karen dreaded it, but the daily exercise was too important a part of her treatment to be skipped or ignored. It was one of the few things that could be done for Karen.

She would never be able to stand or walk. At least, her muscles had to be kept from getting completely atrophied.

Time slipped by as though it were in a hurry. It ran like sand through my fingers. The world seemed naked and gray in the gloomy distance between fall and winter. The trees around the Brown House stretched their branches like black arms toward the sky, as if they were begging for a blanket of snow to hide under. The sky was crisp and transparent. Winter was just around the corner, its chill saturating the air.

We were making almost daily excursions into the countryside. This was one of the last footholds I was stubbornly trying to hold onto. Karen said nothing. Every morning she catatonically let me pull her coat over her rigid arms and wrap a blanket around her legs before I wheeled her slowly across the wide lawn in front of the Brown House. The leaves had turned into a brown, rustling carpet under my feet, sticking to the wheels of Karen's wheelchair. Here and there was a streak of silver across the grass which the frost had left the night before.

I would walk slowly and lazily in order to allow the immaculate serenity of the countryside to envelop us and bring us peace. The forest stood tall and solemn around us, reminiscent of the majesty of a cathedral. This was the only place where our silence did not seem painful or awkward. On the contrary, here it seemed the only right and proper thing.

During our walks through the forest, Karen's face took on a quality of pleasure which I had never seen before. Her eyes seemed to be dancing across the treetops. They were shimmering, dreamy, almost alive. I could never be sure, but every so often I got the impression that she was actually enjoying the scenery and her short freedom from the Brown House.

I was fighting a bittersweet tenderness that was trying to choke me. This little child had already begun to stake out a claim on my heart. She was becoming more and more important to me, despite her efforts to the contrary. Karen was sneaking into my heart and my life. She spread little roots in all directions, clinging there with unyielding tenacity.

All of a sudden it had become very important to reach Karen. It was urgent and necessary. My restlessness grew, giving me no peace. Karen irritated me. She tempted me, the way anything difficult to attain invites to still another effort. Somewhere, deep within me, I knew that I could love this strange little child very much, if she would only let me. But her protective wall was still there, more rejecting and impossible to scale than ever.

I stubbornly forced warmth and kindness out of myself. I squeezed friendliness and compassion out of my soul, almost the same way one would squeeze the last golden drops of juice out of an orange or a lemon. I did it for Karen, because I felt that she needed it. But fatigue had slipped into my voice and tiredness slowed down my movements. Karen's eyes were clear and perceptive. She saw. She understood. But she did not care.

By this time I knew Karen fairly well, at least within the boundaries she had staked out. I had thoroughly explored the grounds she let me enter. I had roamed all around the general, neutral area around her. I knew her little body by heart. I knew which muscles were willing, and which ones had to be forced to obey. I had learned how to help her with her exercises and how to safely support her in the bathtub. I had, by trial and error, finally discovered that she preferred the red dress to the blue.

Practical details. Concrete facts. Worthless effort.

My knowledge was empty and irrelevant. I still had no idea of what was going through Karen's mind. I did not know what she felt or thought, or who she really was behind that cold mask of inaccessibility. Almost six months had passed since we first met.

Fatigue grew in size and strength. It persistently tried to get control over me, and I had to depend more and more heavily on stubbornness to get me through each day.

"I will do it." I said to myself, trying to believe my own words. "I shall find a way, even if it is so narrow and crooked that I can barely walk it. Some day I will have my victory. Some day I will feel her hand seeking mine with trust and comfort, and see the shimmer of a smile in her eyes—"

I will. There is a power in those words. And sometimes prophecy.

"I am worried," the headmistress said. "My conscience is bothering me."

"How come?"

"I'm afraid I have put too great a load on your shoulders. You look pale and tired. You are working too hard."

"If it is Karen you have in mind—"

"You are not getting anywhere, are you?"

"Well, no."

"You see—" she hesitated.

"Yes?"

"No, I don't really know what I wanted to say. It is just that I don't want you to work too hard for something which may be impossible."

"Nothing is impossible," I said with determination. "It may just look that way sometimes."

"You look tired. Do you sleep enough?"

"I'm fine."

She looked at me with her soft, gentle eyes. Her glance was thoughtful and searching and perhaps a little bit worried.

"You have got to understand," I said slowly and carefully. "I am all alone. No strings. No obligations. It's just me. Nobody needs me. Nobody waits for me. Now, here at last I think I have found a place where I might be able to do something with myself. I have found a little girl who needs me—maybe. I am taking a chance, because I have got to try. I cannot just walk away and never know."

The headmistress smiled gently. She too was marked by the bruises of loneliness."

"You see," I said, "I think this is the first time in my life that I have something important to work for."

"God bless you," the headmistress said. "God bless you." Yes, I thought, I hope God would bless me—with a sign of recognition and acceptance from Karen.

The day finally came when fatigue lay so heavy across my chest and the gloominess around me was so intense that I could not fight it any longer. With an irritating, and at the same time pleasant feeling of being defeated, I gave in and allowed the weakness to get hold of me. One morning I stayed at home. I did what I vaguely had been wanting to do for a long time. I looked at at the sky which lay like smoky clouds of cotton across the rooftops. I heard the monotonous song of raindrops against the window. I shook my pillow round and downy and crawled back into the soft embrace the bed was offering me. A drowsy sleepiness ran through my limbs, making me heavy and listless. I enjoyed being helpless, without strength or power. I carelessly pushed duties and responsibilities aside. I was tired. I was sick. I had a legitimate reason for being lazy and selfish.

For several days I lay like that, anchored in the calm, peaceful harbor of illness. My days became gray, dull, tedious. They were completely empty of the stimulating colors of action and activity. My world came to a standstill.

Now and then I felt a mild surprise that the Brown House seemed to be able to carry on without me. Also, even more surprising was the fact that I managed so well without the Brown House. Later I would remember how the thought of not returning entered my feverish mind like a huge, black bird, dangerous and tempting.

Time went on and on. Time, so difficult to catch and so hard to control. I seemed to have too much of it. I did not know what to do with all my empty hours. Too many thoughts about Karen crowded the nothingness of my life.

I missed her. I felt lonely without her. At the same time I knew with painful insight that she was not missing me. Perhaps she was even relieved that I was gone.

I wondered what Karen thought about me. How ridiculous and stubborn I must appear to her! Was she secretly laughing at me? Did she pity me? Was she really as cold and indifferent as she pretended to be? Or did she understand and forgive?

But the questions were too big and had already been asked a hundred times before. It was useless. It was a waste of time. I pushed all the painful questions aside and crawled deeper into my bed, like a child seeking protection from the bogeyman.

The first shivering snowflakes were gently falling that morning when I once again walked across the gravel yard in front of the Brown House. Light, caressing, they danced through the air, touching my cheek like feathery kisses. Winter had finally arrived and was dressing the world as a bride in a veil of snowy lace.

I walked the familiar steps down the hall to the bedrooms and saw Karen sitting there in that crude helplessness that always made me think of a hungry, little sparrow. She turned her head and her dark, mournful eyes looked at me.

I was totally unprepared as I saw her thin face shiver in a sad, hesitant smile.

I wanted to run up to her, take her in my arms, and show her the tears that were burning under my eyelids. But something held me back and warned me not to. I was afraid of scaring her, of shattering that soft, fluttering curve on her lips.

"Hello, Karen," I said awkwardly. My voice was thick and unfamiliar as though it belonged to someone else. In moments of great importance we so often say something completely prosaic. She did not answer. But there was no doubt—she smiled again.

Almost frightened, I turned away. I had to hide my face from the world.

This was the first step on a road which was to be both long and rough. It was a curving, uneven road leading through a strangely dull and gloomy countryside. It would take me on an endless journey through shadowy valleys of despair and sunny meadows of stubborn hope. I was traveling through a barren land searching for something green and growing, searching for a sign of life. But the countryside remained unfruitful, void, a cemetery of disappointments and frustrations.

There were moments when I seriously doubted that I had *ever* seen Karen smile. I was certain that it was nothing but my own imagination, a feverish fantasy, or wishful thinking. I had wanted so very much to see it, and so, maybe I had made myself believe that it had actually happened. One smile does not necessarily mean *two* smiles. Besides, the muscles are so undependably jerky in a cerebral palsied little girl's face. Maybe they were only two emotionless twitches, uncontrollable and meaningless.

My stubborn journey on the long road to "reach" Karen continued in pain and doubt.

Let us take a big step forward. Let us arrive at that crisp winter morning when the snow lay innocently white over the countryside and the sun cast a bleak light from somewhere above the tree-tops.

Karen and I were once again strolling through the forest. The wheelchair was awkward and clumsy in the snow. There was a feeling of peaceful timelessness around us. The trees stood in solemn little groups around us, their naked arms wrapped in a veil of snow and their trunks growing black and rugged from out of the white cover of their feet. The wheelchair moved sluggishly forward. We left a lonely, crooked trail behind us.

Two months had passed since that morning when I had seen Karen smile. We seemed to be back to where we had originally started. I felt as if years had passed since that sparkling, hopeful morning when I first visited the Brown House, so eager and so enthusiastic. What had I accomplished? One smile, two months ago. And nothing, nothing between us since.

Karen was bundled up in the wheelchair. Her cheeks had turned rosy in the frosty air, but her eyes were dark and watchful over the surroundings. I still kept taking her on a walk every morning for some reason I was never quite sure of. Perhaps I wanted to have her to myself. Perhaps I wanted to show her what freedom looked like, and let her experience the beauty and serenity of the unspoiled nature around us.

Whatever my reason, she enjoyed it. Her face would become flushed with suppressed excitement. Her eyes got clearer, larger, and sparkling with life. I would watch her in secret, always careful not to disturb her secret joy. I tried to make our walks lazy, carefree, and long. I would stretch the hours and borrow time. I would steal five minutes, or perhaps even ten, before we had to return to the Brown House.

The snow was creaking and squeaking under the wheelchair. It was stubbornly resisting my efforts to go forward. Finally I stopped.

The silence was endless around us. There was no sound except for the soft rustle of snow falling as a squirrel rushed up into a tree. Karen looked calm and peaceful. Slowly I walked around the wheelchair and kneeled in front of her. I looked right into her thin, ravaged face. Her eyes regarded me apprehensively. Her hands lay strangely still in her lap.

"Karen," I said softly. "Karen—"

Deep within me I knew that nobody can be forced to love. Love cannot be demanded, commanded, or asked for. Yet, at that moment that was exactly what I was doing. My feelings were too strong, and I had lost all desire to be sensible. I reached out and embraced her for the first time.

It was perhaps not so strange, after all. The children in the Brown House were all starving for affection. They needed concrete proof that they were loved. They wanted to sit on your lap while listening to stories, they wanted to come along, hold hands, be close. They needed simple, natural signs of affection. But never Karen. Nobody was allowed to touch her with any form of tenderness. Nobody could come that close to her. I do not even think anybody had ever had the courage to try embracing her. Out of some strange combination of fear and respect she was carefully left alone behind her wall of isolation. That was the way Karen preferred it, or seemed to.

And yet, there we were, Karen and I, in the frosty winter land, and I was lying in the snow by her chair, hugging her desperately, crushingly. She felt painfully thin in my arms. The bitterness and disappointment I had been struggling with for so many months, choked my throat. I felt vulnerable, helpless. For the first time, I was admitting to Karen all the merciless anguish she had brought into my life, and all the pain.

I felt her body stiffen and tighten in my arms. For an instant I wondered where I would hide my face, and where I would take my pain when she rejected me. Then, with a twisted, jerky movement I felt her hand flutter up to my face. She did not push me away as I had expected. She was awkwardly trying to stroke my wet, teary cheek.

Once again she had opened herself up to me. Another little piece of the protective wall had crumbled. There was no longer any doubt. Karen wanted me to need her; she had accepted who I was and the love I wanted to give her.

They say that all progress develops in bits and pieces, uneven and jerky, sometimes taking a step in the wrong direction. This was true also for Karen's progress into the world of giving and loving.

After that winter day she started her long journey back to humanity. It was a slow and painful process, but it was also one that necessarily had to be made. That morning she had taken the first, hesitant step out of her isolation. She had finally mustered the courage to reach out to someone. She had allowed a small part of the invisible wall around her to crumble. Now she had to destroy the rest of it. It was no longer a one-sided battle. We had both taken a gigantic step closer to friendship and trust.

But defeat and adversity were still very much part of the picture and would be for a long time to come.

There was so much to accomplish. There were so many obstacles to conquer. Karen and I were not able to communicate very successfully. Speech was, and would always remain, one of Karen's major challenges. She had tremendous difficulty forming words properly and making the right sounds at the right time. Every muscle in her face was involved in this enormous task. Her body would grow tense and rigid. Her hands fluttered up and down, opening and closing convulsively. Her lips would be moving at random, incomprehensible sounds would sputter forth, some intelligible, most a pathetic gibberish.

Now, finally she was trying to communicate with me. And here I was, hurt and embarrassed because I could not understand her. Her shoulders would droop with disappointment. I felt hollow despair eating my insides. I was furious at my own inability to comprehend. I was miserable about not having the right word for an answer, and sometimes, not having any answer at all.

I tried. I guessed. But too often my reply was the wrong one and each time she knew it. Karen saw right through me. She knew the game I was playing. She understood exactly what I was trying to do. I found that I could not deceive her with guessing games or casual, neutral answers. Still, with a patience I could never quite understand, she forgave me. Perhaps she knew that I was fighting too, to keep up my end of the struggle. Months later our conversations were finally beginning to flow somewhat more smoothly, but it was more of the result of my own developed skill in guessing at what she was trying to say than her own ability to speak.

Speech and vocalization were not Karen's only enemies. Movements, expressions, and gestures were another formidable obstacle. As a rule, the harder Karen tried and the more determination she put into her efforts, the greater was also her failure and the more bitter her disappointment. This is one of the cerebral palsy victim's unfortunate burdens. The more deliberate effort you put into a movement, the more tense and reluctant your muscles become. In their overexcitement, they cannot decide which way to go. There is a short circuit in the conflicting nerve impulses, and finally your hand or foot goes flying in its own, independent direction. It is a merciless battle with many brutal defeats.

Disappointment was our constant companion these days. I was never quite able to understand Karen's drastic change from a frightened little child into an obstinate and courageous young girl. But once she had taken the first, painstaking steps, she refused to give in or turn back. It is possible that she finally realized that this was the only way to relate to the rest of the world. Perhaps she needed to know that she was not fighting alone, but that someone else was willing to support her with faith and confidence, and with a stubbornness as great as her own.

Karen was hesitating and afraid. She was still not completely convinced that the new road she was trying to walk would lead anywhere. However, she was not resisting me any longer. In her own, wavering way she was trying to help and cooperate as best as she could and as best as she dared. We were growing strong together, both in the fight we were sharing and through the inevitable force of endless hours spent together. Eventually she started to laugh occasionally when the wheelchair was sliding across the glassy ice on the winter road through the forest. Every now and then she would use her hands to crudely point out something that caught her attention. She seemed to be listening to the stories I would tell her, and look at the pictures I would draw so patiently.

Every now and then her eyes would follow me with uncertainty and concern as I walked across the floor to talk or play with the other children.

The days passed. Weeks. And months.

For the next several months, while winter occupied the countryside, Karen continued her tedious battle.

It was an endless journey, grueling and tiresome. But she made it with an inch of progress at a time. Little by little, the expression of cool disinterest in her eyes mellowed and gave room for something resembling determination. The look of frightened hostility was slowly replaced by timid curiosity.

For the first time since we had met, Karen seemed to want something. She had finally resolved to do something positive for herself. She wanted to come to grips with all the dark monsters in her soul, conquer them, and keep them at a distance. She was trying to forgive the evil forces of life itself for the crimes that had been committed against her. She was fighting back. It was almost as if all the energy

Karen had used to keep her environment at a distance was now rechanneled into a new direction.

Exercise time was no longer such a frightfully dreaded hour of the day. The foam-rubber pad in the playroom, where she performed her acrobatics, became a challenging arena where rigid muscles and self-determination met head-on. In the beginning, the muscles got their uncontested victories and defeat was written in black letters in the bottoms of her eyes. But as time went by, every so often there were instances when Karen came away the winner. She would smile with satisfaction and carefully glance at me to see if I had noticed. Although I clearly remembered the headmistress's instruction that "effort must always be rewarded," and my praise was abundant, at those times all the encouragement in the world was superfluous and totally unnecessary. Karen herself knew that she had done a good job.

It did not take long for the speech therapist to realize what was happening and use it in her favor. For years, her sessions with Karen had been an exercise in futility. Still, she had tried. She had spent hour after useless hour patiently trying to capture the little girl's attention. Now, at last, she started to get a response. Soon, Karen was an attentive pupil and the lessons increased in frequency. The speech therapist was too dedicated and too professional a woman to let an opportunity such as this slip out of her hands. Often, she made the long trip out to the Brown House on her own time in order to work with Karen. Whenever possible, she would allow me to sit in on the lessons, to learn and observe, so that I would be able to help Karen practice here and there during the day.

Karen was taught how to breathe, and most importantly, how to relax. The speech therapist smiled behind her old-fashioned spectacles and constantly reassured Karen that she need not hurry, or worry, or strain in order to speak. If she would just sit back in her chair and think of sunshine and flowers and all the nice, pretty things in the world, the words would take care of themselves. She was a friendly, well-meaning person whose love for her little charge was unmistakable. I could sense it, and so did Karen. In addition, Karen was beginning to realize the importance of communication as a link to the rest of the world.

It was a long, tedious process, interspersed with constant set-backs and letdowns. But as winter's reign reached its peak outside, and the snow started falling less violently against the window, Karen worked her way through it. She coughed and gasped and blew out imaginary candles. She talked into mirrors and tried to wiggle her tongue. She stuttered. She stammered. She babbled. But she tried.

The speech therapist was a dependable coach whose encouragement and support never failed. I was the cheering section, observing Karen's performance from a front-row seat. I shared her pain each time a sentence sputtered forth muddled and fragmented. My own eyes reflected each failure I could read in Karen's eyes. But then, just as disappointment had grown to menacing proportions and the hope of ever succeeding was beginning to dwindle, she would manage to pronounce a word slowly and clearly enough to understand. That was all it took to send our hopes soaring once again.

Perhaps remembering her training in psychology and motivation principles, the speech therapist ingeniously developed a system which made some communication possible for Karen even without words. It was a system which mostly consisted of eye signals and a few, simple gestures. Bending her head slightly forward meant yes. Closing her eyes meant no. Looking to the side meant I want to leave, or I'm tired. Once the basic code was agreed upon, Karen had a way of responding to those questions which did not need an elaborate answer.

I was never able to figure out if it was part of the speech therapist's scheme all along, but it seemed as if having this signaling system to fall back upon took some of the pressure off Karen. The very idea that she did not have to speak, made it easier for her. She relaxed somewhat, and as a result she was able to talk better.

Although Karen never learned to speak with complete ease and fluency, she made great progress and gradually established a line of communication with her environment. I learned too. The hours I spent observing the speech therapist and listening to Karen's attempts to speak eventually gave me an idea of how to best formulate questions, what time to choose, what words Karen was most likely to use, and how they sounded when they frequently got all tangled up into one another.

It was a difficult lesson for us all to learn, but one which love and persistence ultimately helped us master to fair satisfaction. Communication was important to both of us. Karen wanted to be able to make herself understood. I wanted to talk to her and to listen to what she had to say. Ardently, we both worked at it during that long, tiresome winter.

By the time the first signs of spring hesitantly appeared, we were doing pretty well.

Easter was approaching, and the Brown House came alive with hurry and precipitation.

The snow was still protecting the ground, but coarser now, and soggier. It was no longer a downy, white blanket, but a dull, gray mud that soon would trickle away and leave room for the faint beginning of spring.

The sun was still a bleak, white circle outside the window, forming squares of brightness on the floor in the playroom. Somebody had cut a twig off a willow and its tiny buds were bursting into a bashful green. The sound of squeaking wheelchairs and thumping crutches had taken on a tone of anticipation and restlessness. The twittering little voices were eager and shrill.

The children would soon be leaving for home. Only three of them would remain in the quiet embrace of the brown House during Easter. Karen was one of them.

Our relationship had gradually become warmer, more meaningful, and less complicated. During the long winter months, Karen had steadfastly kept up her quiet battle. Little by little, she had come out of her shell. She had slowly and cautiously joined the rest of the family in the Brown House. She revealed a quiet, shy, and humble personality which still bore evidence of scars and bruises. But after nine months of daily togetherness, she was finally beginning to trust me.

I had become her friend, at last. I was her comforter and her tower of strength when she needed it. There were moments when she would cling to me with a fear and despair so great that I could almost feel it within myself. It was a great responsibility.

By this time we were able to communicate quite comfortably. As time went by we had developed a system of guessing and gesturing that finally had become polished to mutual satisfaction. Her speech had improved, and so had my skill at listening and guessing. She used her hands as much as it was possible and as often as they were willing to obey her commands. Whenever her hands failed to communicate her thoughts, she would use her eyes, for signaling, pointing, and indicating.

Our relationship was no longer empty and dead with silence. It had taken a great step forward into a new phase. Sound and communication now filled our time together. We had so much to talk about, so much to share. And so much lost time to make up.

I had finally reached my goal. All the struggle, the waiting, the disappointments now seemed worthwhile. Karen was no longer just a remote, unreachable child. She was *my* Karen—my sister, my daughter, my friend.

The headmistress had a look of disbelief about her. But Karen was now a vital, sharing member of the Brown House.

Easter finally came and the Brown House became quiet and empty. Most of the children had left. Only three of the little ones stayed behind.

Karen sat in the hallway, watching them leave. I did not have much time for her that afternoon. I was running around, locking suitcases, greeting parents, and kissing children good-bye. The Brown House was a caldron containing a magic brew concocted from hurry, disorder, and confusion. Joy was whirling in the air. Laughter filled every room. Expectation greeted each car that drove up to the front door. The children were looking forward to seven glorious days of freedom during the Easter vacation. Filled with happiness, they were leaving.

When dusk came creeping across the lawn they were gone and the Brown House relaxed in a strangely empty silence.

Exhausted I sat down on the bottom step of the wide stairway. My body was aching and my mind was numb from movement and hurry. The hallway looked strangely bare and deserted. Left in the lonely embrace of the Brown House were three forgotten little ones. This day they had been forced to experience the most painful form of loneliness. They had been forced to witness joy, excitement and anticipation but were not able to share these pleasures. They had seen love but none for them to share.

I had to go and find Karen. I wondered where she was. But my mind was so weary and my limbs so heavy that any form of movement seemed impossible.

I thought about the children that had left and felt concerned about the ones that had been left behind. These poor little souls seemed to have an endless path of loneliness ahead of them. They would never get away from this situation. They would always be left behind, because there was no place for them to go. There was no place where they were wanted. Would they ever get used to it? Perhaps. Their rejection would eventually become a scar that would not hurt quite as much as it hurt them right now. Life for them would always be cruel, and I cried inside thinking about the endless loneliness that lay ahead for them.

I had not noticed Karen, but my thoughts were suddenly shattered by her voice. She had been sitting partly hidden behind the stairway, watching me. There was a guarded expression on her face which reminded me of her old hostility. She understood what I was thinking. By now, we knew each other well enough so that certain things were inevitable and could not be disguised. I knew that she knew.

"Why are you sad?" she said slowly and carefully, although she already knew the answer.

"I am tired," I replied.

Her eyes regarded me watchfully.

"Are you sad because they left?" she wondered.

"Sure. Everything seems so different when the house is quiet and empty like this. You know, this place is always so full of noise and laughter that it seems very strange not to see children everywhere. Don't you think so, too? Imagine everybody taking off like that?"

"Not everybody," Karen said with brutal logic.

"Thank heavens for that," I sighed. "I wouldn't have been too happy to see you leave, Karen."

A quick smile flashed across her face as though these words carried some importance to her. After a long silence and great difficulty forming the words, Karen continued.

"I am always here."

How do you respond to a statement like that? What do you say to a child like Karen? I had no reply to give her.

"Did you want to leave, too?"

Karen shrugged.

"Listen, Karen. I am really very pleased that the other children left because that means that you and I will have so much more time all to ourselves."

The shadows under her eyes were deep and violet. She eats too little, I thought to myself.

"This week we are going to do all the things that we
have never been able to do when everybody else is around.
We can spend hours in the forest, if you like, and there
won't be anybody telling us what time to be back."

She looked at me seriously.

"Say, why don't we start right now? Let's sneak into
the kitchen and see what we can find in the refrigerator.
Maybe we'll even have a picnic at the kitchen table."

The wheelchair squeaked in the vast silence as we
crossed the hallway to the kitchen. I stroked Karen lightly
over the hair.

"How are you feeling?" I asked.

She stared into her lap.

"I don't know," she whispered. "I am not really sad. I
just feel kind of funny."

Those seven days of Easter vacation, with uninterrupted strolls through the countryside and lazy afternoons
in the complacent stillness of the playroom, brought us
very close together. I was beginning to feel that I finally
had reached Karen. There was no longer any rejection or
hostility. There was no longer any mystery or any piece
missing in the jigsaw puzzle which formed Karen, Or, so it
would seem. . . .

We were sitting in the early morning silence of the playroom, talking lazily to each other. The first thin rays of
bleak sunshine were cautiously creeping up on the window-
sill, making the headmistress's little canary sing with rap-
ture in his cage. His joyful warbling rose and sank in the

stillness of the Brown House that was still in sleepy repose. From the kitchen came distant breakfast noises and a tempting aroma of bacon and freshly made coffee.

Karen was leaning back in her chair, her head tilted slightly to one side and her hands trembling in her lap.

"Isn't it strange," she said.

"What?"

"That we can think and talk to each other."

"Well, don't you think that is nice?"

"Oh, yes, but how does it actually happen?"

Karen's mind was sharp and inquisitive.

"Oh dear, those things are so complex that I don't think anybody really knows for sure."

"What does 'complex' mean?"

"Hard, difficult."

She regarded me solemnly. In her dark eyes I could see a fleeting glimpse of that mournful sadness that seemed to be a part of Karen, that never completely disappeared.

"Why are things difficult? Do they have to be?"

That was one of those monumental questions which children so often, and with such ease, put to us grown-ups, expecting an immediate and simple answer.

Well, I tried. "Just think for a minute, Karen. If nothing in life were hard or difficult, then that would mean that everything would be easy and comfortable all the time, right?"

She nodded. "That would be nice."

I wanted so much to agree with her, but of course I could not admit it.

"Come on, now. You know very well that it wouldn't be nice for very long. If you were always cheerful and happy and things were always going your way day in and day out, then pretty soon you would wake up one morning and discover that you didn't really know what 'happy' meant any more. You see, you wouldn't have anything else to compare it with. You would get used to it and start taking it for granted. If there isn't anything sad there cannot be anything happy, and if there isn't anything difficult there cannot be anything easy."

She agreed.

"You see, Karen, it may seem odd, but it is very clever, really. Just think about it. It is absolutely necessary to feel sad now and then in order to know how to feel happy."

She looked serious. So terribly serious.

"But why are some people sad almost all the time?"

"Tell me, who is sad almost all the time?"

She looked away, and all of a sudden I knew. It was so difficult to talk to Karen sometimes. With that natural honesty most children have, she uncovered the truth crudely and abruptly. Many a time she caught me without an answer, and it did not only hurt her but myself as well. Like children everywhere, she seemed to think that just because I was several years older than she is, it must also necessarily follow that I possessed all the answers. There were no answers. I did not have them, nor did anybody else.

"Listen, Karen," I said tenderly. "I think I know what you are talking about. But you see, some people only pretend to be happy sometimes, when they are really very sad."

She did not say anything.

"I get sad too, sometimes."

"I know," she said plainly.

"You know?"

"Your eyes get sad."

I was beginning to feel uneasy. I had to end this conversation somehow, turn it away from all the sadness and onto a happier, more positive note.

"There is one thing I am very happy about, though. Can you guess what?"

She shook her head silently.

"I am happy that I know a sweet, pretty little girl like you!"

But Karen had become gloomy all of a sudden.

"Lisa is pretty—"

"Why, so are you!"

"Nobody else thinks so."

I reached out and embraced her. If I could not comfort her with words, I had to try to soothe her sadness away in my arms.

"Oh, Karen," I said. "My little girl."

She leaned her head against my shoulder, making herself more comfortable in my embrace. She sat there for a moment, apparently content with the comfort I was offering. Then suddenly she spoke.

"I wish you were my mother."

I was surprised, but flattered. It felt good to hear her say that. Still, my reply was inevitable.

"But I'm not, you know. Not really. It only feels that way sometimes. For me, too—"

"Do you know my mother?"

"No, I'm afraid not."

"I wonder what she is like."

"She is probably very nice."

"Why?"

"I don't know, but how else could she have a wonderful little girl like you?"

Karen was silent for a little while. Finally, the words came out with great difficulty.

"Then how come she doesn't want me?"

It hurt to hear her say it.

"Your mother cannot take care of you properly. You know how much trouble we are having with your exercises every day, and how tired we both get sometimes."

"She could come and visit. Or write."

"You know, Karen, I'm sure your mother is just as unhappy that she cannot be with you as you are about not being with her."

She pulled away and looked at me in surprise.

"But I don't want to. I don't want to be with her at all!"

"Do you . . ."

"I don't like her! I don't ever want to see her!" she insisted vehemently.

"But you don't even know her."

"I don't care. I don't want her anyway. I want a mother who comes to visit and plays with me and hugs me. That's what a mother is supposed to do, isn't it?"

The tears were beginning to well up in her eyes. I was wondering if it was more from hurt or from anger.

For a long time we sat with our arms wrapped around each other. She was crying quietly against my shoulder while I was trying to figure out exactly what a mother is supposed to be.

"Don't cry, Karen. I'm here. I'll stay as long as you need me and want me to."

A mother is somebody to cling to and trust. A mother is a warm, secure shelter of warmth and protection, in whose arms you can always hide and be as little and scared as you want to be. A mother is love and understanding, no matter what you do or how you look. A mother is strength, wisdom, and love. A mother is supposed to be so many things that she does not always have the power or ability to be. I tried to be as much of a mother as I could for Karen, tried to be the mother she did not have—and I thought of my own mother who also abandoned me.

I felt so sorry for Karen who suffered so much. And, in spite of it all, I felt sorry for Karen's mother who was so severely judged by her sick and crippled child.

Through this fragmented conversation and a thousand others just like it, my understanding of Karen grew. I was not surprised at the desperate hostility she expressed toward her mother. To a certain extent I shared her feelings. Karen was starving for all the comforting love most mothers provide their children. She missed the security of a strong, central figure in her life and was painfully aware of her own loneliness. True, I was there, and so was the headmistress and her staff. But at nineteen years of age I was really more of a friend than a mother, and the headmistress's responsibilities were too numerous to allow the time that would have been necessary to give Karen the special mothering she needed.

Karen needed another interest, because too often there were times when she seemed to indulge in her misery, enlarging her problems until they became immense and insurmountable. She needed something that would fit smoothly into her life, holding her attention and capturing her thoughts. It would have to be some sort of hobby which could be enjoyed in spite of her physical limitations and her naturally introverted disposition. It would have to be something which would make her forget about herself from time to time and would ease the painful burden of her bitter loneliness. She needed diversion in her life, a sense of usefulness, and a feeling of satisfaction.

What I did not know was that Karen herself had already found an interest which perfectly suited all her needs and purposes. She gave to it a complete and glorious devotion. It was something of such enormous importance that it had to be kept a secret—from the world, from the Brown House, even from me.

There was no way I possibly could have guessed.

Part Two

Part Two

Let us take another great step forward. Let us hurry to meet the other main actor in this drama—Elvis Presley.

For a long time I never even realized that he was part of the cast, in a role that was more prominent than anybody else's. He waited patiently to enter the scene, and to give strength and beauty to Karen's eye. His sudden entrance baffled me, and yet, I do not know what I would have done without him.

A person can be great in so many ways: strength, talent, wealth. Here those accomplishments are all irrelevant. Elvis was great because he possessed kindness and generosity, compassion and goodness. He was a man with a heart so big that in spite of his talent, wealth, and fame, he still found time and room to give of himself to Karen, one of God's smallest, saddest little children.

Karen and I came in from outside where a gentle warmth had come into the air. We had once again been strolling far away into the unknown corners of the country-side, exploring the bright land of almost-spring. The wheel-chair was squeaking its way across the soggy lawn and into the safe belly of the Brown House. We were welcomed by the warm smell of baking bread and the shrill noise of a garrulous record player.

The Easter week was coming to an end. This was our last day alone in the Brown House before the rest of the children would be returning from their vacations. As a special treat, we indulged in hot chocolate and freshly baked rolls at the kitchen table. Karen's eyes were soft and dreamy over the steaming cup. She still loved our walks through the serene countryside surrounding the Brown House. She constantly wanted to explore new roads, see different houses and strange people. Little by little, we had expanded our boundaries and ventured into new and foreign territory miles away from the Brown House. Every day opened a new horizon for Karen, bringing her a little more knowledge about the appearance of the outside world.

The house was filled with music. The noise was pleasantly loud and shrill. It was a joyous sound that enlivened the stillness of the Brown House.

For some reason or other, my duties called me away and I had to leave Karen alone for a few minutes. As always, I detected a trembling prayer in her eyes: do not leave me alone for too long, and do not go too far away.

But I was caught up in irrelevancies and almost an hour passed before I hurried to join Karen again. I expected to see her big eyes turn worriedly toward me, asking me silently what had taken so long. But for once I was wrong. She was sitting just the way I had left her, lost in her faraway thoughts. Her lips were pouting just slightly, and there was a hint of a frown between her eyes. She startled as I came up behind her.

"Hey, what are you dreaming about?"

She stirred and nodded toward the record player.

"Nothing. I'm listening."

Karen loved music. We would sit for hours by the radio or the record player. She was tireless. Invariably, her body would relax, allowing her spastic limbs to find a moment of repose and comfort. Her expression would become tender and distant. She was like somebody gingerly floating away in a daydream.

The afternoon went by in quiet peacefulness. Karen was engaged in the music and I busied myself by watching her listen. I wonder if anybody ever gets tired of regarding the face of someone they love.

Karen's face was emaciated and marked by suffering and grief. Her eyes were enormous and painted with the dark colors of loneliness and despair. The deep hollows in her cheeks made her look undernourished and sickly. Her most attractive asset was her hair, which fell in silky, brown disorder over her shoulders.

It was apparent that she was enjoying the music, drinking each note with an insatiable thirst. Her eyes were on the sky outside the window, dancing across the treetops in dreamy flight to some remote paradise where the Brown House no longer existed.

From time to time I thought I detected a slight tremor hurrying across her face. She looked as if she was trying to suppress some secret excitement. She listened more intensely, more attentively. At first I was sure that I was mistaken. I thought it was nothing but her spastic, quivering muscles playing a trick on me. But as the afternoon wore on, there seemed to be more to it than that. It was some form of deliberate tension. She was in deep concentration. She appeared to be straining her whole body in order to hear better.

Funny, I thought. I had never noticed it before. What was she thinking? What made her expressions change so rapidly? She did not even seem to be aware of it herself. I did not understand. But the afternoon was cozy and I dismissed all questions from my mind.

Slowly, the day passed and night came. Every now and then I noticed the same tense apprehension in Karen's face but did not pay too much attention to it. We finished our evening routine as usual. It gave me a sense of usefulness to help this little child with all the tasks she could not handle by herself. I enjoyed knowing how to do it, being able to do it, and now, at last, being permitted to do it. At last she was bathed, brushed, and tucked into the soft embrace of the bed. I sat by her side for a few minutes before turning out the lights. She was eagerly showing me her precious collection of bubble-gum cards. They were photographs of famous men and women that came with popular packs of pink gum. It was one of her few treasures which she kept carefully hidden in her nightstand drawer.

She held the brittle little cards carefully between her rigid fingers, stubbornly refusing all my offers to help. She was proud of her collection. She showed me each card again and again, and naturally I was duly impressed. Her eyes were glowing with excitement as she examined them, one by one. Some just a little longer than the rest.

A little while later, as night was clasping its dark and soothing hand around the world, I tiptoed back to Karen's bedroom. The Brown House lay drowsy and relaxed around me, enveloped in that strange stillness it had known for the past week. Tomorrow the children would return with their happy noise and cheerful confusion. Our time of splendid privacy was over. It had been a good week, I thought complacently as I walked down the hallway. We had passed the difficult part of the road, and from here on our journey would be smooth and easy. With motherly instinct, I just wanted to check on Karen and make sure that she was all right before I left for the night.

I stopped in her doorway and was frightened at what I saw.

Karen was huddling in her bed, her body stiff in merciless rigidity. Her head was trembling. She was clenching the pillow in her arms, pressing it desperately against her face so as not to let any betraying sound escape into the stillness of the night. She was crying, desperately and violently.

I stood aghast, completely baffled. Nothing made sense. Only a short while ago everything had been in perfectly normal order, or so it had seemed. I had left her smiling sleepily in the warm comfort of the bed. Still, here she was, barely one-half hour later, her thin body distorted with twisted grief.

What had happened? Had she hurt herself? Was she in pain? Had she had a nightmare? Was she afraid of the dark or unusual, empty silence of the deserted Brown House? No, Karen was not so easily frightened by either silence or darkness. She was not able to move around enough to have hurt herself. Besides, she was too well acquainted with physical pain to let it conquer her like this. Somehow I sensed that this was a different kind of pain, much greater and more powerful. But what? Why?

"Karen," I whispered. "Oh, Karen, Karen . . ."

My mind was bursting with questions, but for some reason I did not ask them. I just sat by her side, awkwardly caressing her forehead and saying meaningless words which were meant to soothe and comfort. I wanted to run and drag the headmistress out of bed, but at the same time I was afraid of leaving Karen alone, even for a few minutes. Her body was trembling in spastic convulsions. Her hands were clenched tight around the pillow. Weeping shook her little body, vehemently and without mercy. But not a sound came from her lips. I was bewildered. I was terrified.

Minutes dragged by, perhaps hours. After what felt like an eternity, her crying slowly stopped. Her body relaxed and she fell asleep with her face still buried in the damp pillow. Even in sleep her muscles would still quiver occasionally, weary from the strenuous ordeal they had just been through.

Long after her breathing had finally become peaceful and regular, I remained by her side. My heart was aching with sadness and pity. My thoughts were spinning in endless circles. All of a sudden I felt almost as small and helpless as Karen herself.

My concept of Karen had suddenly been shattered into a million pieces. I had been so sure that I knew her. I had felt confident that I had explored all the corners of her mind and thoughts. Obviously, I must have been wrong. I must have overlooked something. My understanding of her was not complete after all. There were still pieces missing.

What in the world could have caused her such devastating pain? I was torn apart by compassion and by my own inadequacy. I had come to love Karen very much and somehow my love for her made my inability to help her now seem so much greater. My thoughts led me nowhere except into chaos.

Finally I got up to leave her, my mind dull with fatigue. Carefully I bent down to kiss her on the cheek. That is when I saw it. One of the little bubble-gum cards that we had been looking at earlier in the evening was rigidly clasped in her stiff little hand. In the dim light I saw the face of a dark, solemn young man. It was the face of Elvis Presley.

Gracefully, destiny had handed me the missing piece. I now understood Karen completely and realized why she had cried herself to sleep.

With the photograph in my hand, I searched my way through the sleeping Brown House to the deserted playroom. All of a sudden I remembered Karen's expression of apprehension earlier that afternoon. Thoughtfully, and still not quite certain of what I was looking for, I searched through the pile of records by the record player. The idea was still obscure and uncertain, but I was beginning to detect something which might be a clue to Karen's sadness.

Here and there among the colorful record covers were albums by Elvis Presley.

Could it be possible?

I was standing in front of a window display in a record store, confusedly turning the thought over and over in my mind.

I looked at Elvis's face in front of me, so strangely serious. It was enlarged in a huge, blown-up photograph in the center of the window. His eyes were dark and dreamy. His lips were generous and pouting just slightly. His hands looked strong and tender at the same time. He was very definitely a sensuous man. I had heard that women of all ages went into hysterics while watching him perform. I wondered how a man with such a serious-looking face could have such a devastating power.

What did Karen feel for him? Did she feel nothing at all? I realized that I might be mistaken, but somehow I did not think so.

Could it be possible? It was a theory which could easily be put to the test, an idea which could be proved correct or incorrect.

Finally, after one last glance at Elvis's face, I entered the music store and bought a record. It was a flat, black little disc on which his voice was forever preserved. From the record cover his eyes looked back at me. Dark. Captivating. Sultry.

It never occurred to me that I might hurt Karen. Not until much later did I realize the chance I was taking and the possible dangers connected with what I was about to do. Perhaps I was lucky. Destiny directed me so cleverly that hesitation never got in my way.

Karen was waiting for me. As I crossed the lawn in front of the Brown House, I could see her sitting by the window in the hallway. She was looking for me. Her pale face was colored with anxious wondering as to why I was gone. When she finally caught sight of me, a hesitating smile slowly made its way across her lips. She looked relieved.

"What's that?" She nodded toward the package under my arm.

"It's a present for you."

I wheeled her down to the bedroom. At this moment we needed to be alone, without an audience. I felt that nobody had the right to watch Karen, should it prove that my vague suspicion was right. I did not know exactly what sort of reaction I was expecting, but with some obscure, instinctive intuition I felt that we might be facing a moment of importance and revelation.

Karen had not received many gifts in her life. She was not quite sure of the proper way to behave on an occasion like this. She was blushing with excitement. Her hands were flying about, uncontrollable, as always when she was filled with emotion. Slowly and carefully I helped her remove the ribbon and the pretty wrapping paper. At last . . .

It was a shock to her. I knew it the instant she saw Elvis's face on the record. All at once it was written in capital letters across her face. She had never expected anybody to find out. But here she was with her glorious secret cruelly and carelessly brought out into the open. It had been brutally exposed by someone she had finally learned to trust. I could see the confusion in her face and felt myself grow numb with fear all of a sudden. In a flash of naked truth, I realized what a cruel, clumsy fool I had been. With one careless, thoughtless gesture I was destroying everything it had taken me so much time and effort to create. Our friendship had come to an end. I had lost her, right there and then. I knew that after this nothing could follow.

My vague suspicion had been correct, after all. But there was more to it than that. Despite Karen's desperate crying the previous night, I had failed to see the magnitude of her secret love. The glory of it. The importance. My crude efforts to do good had shattered it to pieces, exposed her dream to the world. It was no longer specially hers. My knowledge of it had robbed her of the one joy that was hers alone.

She was bewildered and shocked. The muscles were tight little knots under her skin. Her eyes were anxiously flickering back and forth over the record, her own quivering hands, and the wrapping paper that we had carelessly tossed on the floor. Then, at last, she dared to look at me.

She had to find out whether it was all coincidence, or if I really knew. Her dark eyes scanned my face for a sign. I could see that she was scared. It was a moment of chaos.

I knew that I had to say something. It was up to me now. Somehow I had to find the right words that would make her understand. I had to do something that would set everything straight again. I could not afford to lose her. But my crude failure was already a fact. My error was committed. There were no words great or powerful enough to erase my clumsiness.

"Karen," I whispered. "Oh Karen, please forgive me—"

My voice was strangely unfamiliar. I was fighting back the tears that were trying to choke me. Awkwardly, I tried to embrace her, hoping to assure myself that through some strange miracle we still belonged together in a wonderous friendship greater than most people ever come to know.

But Karen pushed me away with a forceful, spastic jerk and her eyes were cold as she looked at me.

"Karen," I said humbly. "Please let me explain."

Elvis regarded us from the record cover. His eyes seemed to see what was happening between Karen and me, and his eyes understood; they seemed to overflow with pity and compassion.

"Why did you give me this?" Karen asked with extreme difficulty.

I just shook my head.

"Why?" she insisted.

"I wanted to give you a present."

"But why? Why *this*?"

"Well," I tried. "You like music, don't you? And—and I thought—"

It did not sound very convincing.

"You see," I tried in desperation, "I have always admired this man, and—"

My words were hollow and false. Even I did not believe them.

"Oh, damn it, Karen!" I blurted out. "What's the use? I never paid much attention to him at all until last night when I saw you crying. Then all of a sudden it dawned upon me that perhaps there was somebody that meant very much to you, without my knowing about it. I mean, somebody that was very special to you. I wasn't sure and I didn't know how to ask you. I—I thought that perhaps you didn't even want me to know about it, or perhaps that you would tell me about it sometime in the future. But then, I—Well, you see, I love you very much, Karen. I hope you know that by now. So, I said to myself, if this man means something to Karen then I would like to make her happy and give her one of his records. I wasn't going to ask you anything, Karen. I wasn't going to tell anybody else about it. I just wanted you to be happy. I never mean to get you upset or hurt you. I'm sorry that it happened. I'm sorry. I really am."

I stopped. All of a sudden I had nothing more to say. At last I had succumbed to the truth and told her the simple, naked facts which suddenly seemed so crude and so awkward.

I felt drained. There was nothing more to add. I had used too many words already, pouring them over her in a jerky, stupid way. I did not know if she understood. I did not even know if she had been listening. I wondered if she sensed all the desperate, remorseful love that was behind my words.

"I see," Karen said softly.

I was waiting for her to go on, to continue, to say something that would release the trembling tension in the air. But she remained silent. She was still now, thoughtfully composed in a great calm. Her eyes were resting on Elvis's solemn face. Her fingers fluttered gently across his eyes, his cheek, his lips, in a tender caress. She appeared pensive, a faint smile playing on her lips.

Suddenly she looked up, searching my face thoughtfully.

"Do you really love me like you said?" she asked bluntly.

"Do you really have to ask me that?"

"But I mean, *really?*"

"Yes, I do. Really."

She smiled faintly.

"Do you want to know something?" she asked carefully.

"Yes, I would. That is, if you feel that you want to tell me."

Karen sighed deeply. Her eyes hurried across Elvis's features on the record cover, as though she wanted to ask his permission and consent. It was a breathless moment. I expected the world to shatter into a million little pieces in front of my eyes, but through some strange miracle it did not.

"You see—" Karen began. And I learned that night how much she adored Elvis Presley.

I learned how his voice comforted her suffering. How it calmed her heart that was trembling in its longing for beauty and love. Once she had found Elvis, she nourished him with the sweet fruits of limitless, secret love. She gave him the devotion of a child, clean, pure, and innocent. He did not betray her humble offer. He stayed in her heart and gave her in return hope, meaning, and fulfillment.

Hours later I lay on my bed, absentmindedly exploring the smooth white of the ceiling. The puzzle was complete, at last. All the odd little pieces now fit together evenly and freely, forming a clear, logical pattern. The center piece sparkled with importance. Elvis gave life and meaning to the picture. He was the light of hope and joy against the background of despair and solitude in Karen's life.

Somebody said that without love humanity could not exist. Nobody can live in a world of nothingness. No one accepts a fate of barren desperation without trying to change it just a little. A suffering little child does not survive in this gloomy world without creating some sort of consolation and escape, even if only in a dream about a great man.

Suddenly everything seemed to make sense. It was really very simple. He was the one aspect of her life that was perfect. The Brown House, in spite of its friendliness, still bore the inevitable characteristics of an institution. The doctors, the therapists, and the nurses were always hurrying, always in search of more time. The other children in the Brown House tried with generous patience but still never quite understood Karen's guttural speech or uncontrolled gestures. First and last, there were the parents who did not want her. Everyone and everything failed Karen except Elvis Presley.

She faced a life of dull pain and sad, gray hopelessness. I tried to imagine her feelings when she discovered that most people have bodies that were not only healthy and even beautiful, but also functioning, well working, and obedient. And then, to realize that she was an exception, a misfit, a defective piece of machinery, and a burden for those on whom you were forced to rely. But the cruelty and injustice did not end there. The final blow to her lively, curious mind had to be the realization that her fate was irrevocable, that things would never change, that nothing could be done. Ever.

I tried to put myself in Karen's situation and asked myself what I would have done, and whether I would have had the strength to endure. I know I could not have managed alone. But even Karen did not bear her agony in solitude. She had the invisible support of two gracious and powerful friends: the good Lord and Elvis Presley.

I still wonder how her love for Elvis all began.

With a picture, perhaps? A song? A vague remark by somebody else? Maybe his voice touched a sensitive nerve in Karen's ear. Perhaps her eyes sauntered casually across a picture of his face and she never forgot it. There was an eternity of possibilities, yet they all had two characteristics in common: casualness and chance.

Karen herself did not seem to know. When I carefully asked how long Elvis had been with her and how they had made their initial acquaintance, she could not find an answer. Instead, she looked at me with surprised annoyance, as if that were a question I should know better than to ask, or perhaps one she had never stopped to ask herself. With a feeling of having somehow been untactful, I left it alone. I was never to find out for sure. Although the question bothered me and would pop into our conversation again and again in various forms during the long months to come, Karen never had a satisfactory answer. She would just look at me in a way that made me realize that how and when she first discovered Elvis was utterly irrelevant. All that really mattered was that he was there, a part of her life, and that the feelings she felt for him comforted her.

It was love. There was no question about it. Love in its purest, cleanest, most devoted form. Limitless and all-encompassing.

And he was strikingly handsome—even I could see that. The dark and dreamy eyes, the sultry and slightly pouting lips. And there was a bold masculinity about him that was both mysterious and appealing. Karen readily admitted that he was "the best-looking man she had ever seen." She had not seen that many men in her life, and she was only nine, but I still wondered if Elvis had not touched the very first stirrings of the femininity within her.

But there was more to it than that. "He is a very sad person," Karen had said, and sadness was something she could easily identify with. And, indeed as I looked into his face and listened to his voice, I knew what she was talking about. There was a strange, undertone of sadness behind the lyrics, that seemed to be coming straight out of his soul. I knew that he, too, had lost his mother and never had been able to quite get over it. Perhaps Karen was right. She was only a child, but her sensitivity and intuition had the depths of one who had lived to a ripe, old age. I decided that yes, sadness was the common bond that bound Karen and Elvis together.

At the same time, he displayed some very opposite qualities which were equally appealing to Karen. The reckless abandon of some of his songs, the fast pace, and the arrogant delivery both excited and tempted her. It was a frightening, exhilarating feeling for a little girl who never had had an opportunity to jump in and enjoy life headfirst. It must have been very much like one's first ride on a roller coaster, I thought to myself. You are petrified, and love every minute of it.

There was another question, too, about which I frequently speculated. Elvis was famous for his activity on the stage: his gyrations, his suggestive movements, his trembling legs. I asked myself how much influence all this physical activity from the waist down had on a little girl confined to a wheelchair. Was this one of the reasons that he was singled out and blessed with all her love?

But all these conjectures really did not matter. What mattered was that she had found him, whatever the reason. He sustained her. He was important.

Fate had brought Elvis into Karen's life and he had found his way to her lonely spirit. Karen's heart was scarred by loneliness and bruised by despair. It cried out for someone to soothe her pain, someone to light a sparkle of warmth. Someone to fill her empty days with peace and love and meaning.

Elvis was goodness personified. At first he approached her dimly, like a shadow, lacking a figure or shape. In the beginning he was intangible. But during the long hours of her infinite loneliness, he started to come alive. Slowly he acquired size and form. As time went by, his personality emerged, and later his convictions and beliefs. He proved to be all the things she secretly longed and wished for. In her relentless hunger for love, she made Elvis Presley a powerful human being, comprised of all the things she so painfully missed in her own life. He represented the sheltered security of parental care. He symbolized the dependable loyalty of true friendship. He became the warmth of affection and the comfort of understanding. He lent her a helping hand through her worst moments of grief and distress. He occupied the secret stage of her dreams and thoughts. He taught her the bittersweet pleasures of distant, secret love. He was hope, faith, and fulfillment. He was life itself.

In my collection of memories, the quiet afternoon when Karen so solemnly brought her personal Elvis into my life sparkles with greater clarity and importance than our times together before. Our introduction was tender and soft-spoken.

Karen's words were soft but full of formidable emotion. Her eyes sparkled with graceful beauty as she opened the door to her heart's innermost chamber and let me see all the brittle, hopeful dreams that were buried there. Her face was serious and thoughtful. Her fingertips followed the gentle curve of Elvis's lips on the record cover in absent-minded tenderness. And in the midst of my vast bewilderment, I made another unbelievable discovery: for the first and only time in her life, I saw Karen's body in complete relaxation. Her speech was even controlled. Her hands lay limp and graceful in her lap. The spasticity was miraculously gone, and for some divine, inexplicable reason, it stayed that way for almost two full hours that we spent talking.

The good Lord had graciously given me a hint, which to my amazement, had proven to be correct. To show me the importance of the task he was assigning me, he was now performing a physical miracle right in front of my eyes. I felt as if I were being taken by the hand and shown a strange and winding road which I knew that I faithfully must follow.

A child needed me. With quiet humility, Karen was inviting me to share her glorious secret. With faithful trust, she told me about Elvis. With unquestioned confidence and childish innocence she placed her heart gently in my hands, to protect, to save, and to nourish.

For a moment I trembled, painfully aware of my own shortcomings. I desperately hoped that God knew what he was doing, and that he would remember to support me as I stumbled along in the serious assignment he had given me. My thoughts went to Elvis. How strange . . . At that very moment, he lived his busy life on the opposite side of the globe, completely unaware of the important role he played in our lives. Karen loved him. She loved him out of deep, desperate need, as much as any nine-year-old girl was ever able to love. Intuitively, I knew that it was now my responsibility to make sure that her emotions, her dreams and her hopes were kept alive, safely protected and carefully hidden from possible damage from the outside world.

I knew that the outside world does not always share our individual opinions about what is important and what is not. I felt that perhaps it would not so readily accept the fact that there are instances when nothing really matters except for a child's unrealistic, impossible dream. Better then, not to let them know.

Thus, I kept my discoveries quiet and buried Karen's secret in the safest place I could find: the hidden depths of my own heart.

The afternoon when I first made Elvis's acquaintance through Karen's eyes is with me still. I shall never forget the precious moment when, for the first time in my life, I was allowed to share the secret confidence of a child who had discovered the transforming power of love.

Easter was over and the children had returned. The Brown House had resumed its friendly atmosphere of cheerful noise and cozy disorder. Once again the air was bubbling with eager little voices, pounding crutches, and squeaking wheelchairs. Reluctantly, we returned to schedule and routine. My plentiful excess of time vanished and the precious moments with Karen shrank. Still, our relationship was close and intimate, and suddenly full of the sweet thrills of sharing a secret.

Elvis entered my life with persuasive determination.

He took one step at a time. Each day Karen brought me another little piece of his personality. It did not take him long to assume the appearance of a friend, and I quickly learned to accept him as an integral and inevitable part of my life. His strange entrance into my life still puzzled me. Yet, there were moments when I reached out to him with profuse gratitude for his presence.

Once Karen had introduced me to Elvis, she was overcome by forceful desire to have me get to know him better. With zealous determination she told me the story about Elvis—his early childhood, his accidental discovery, and his rise to stardom. She knew his life story by heart, but it did not stop there. She knew his character, his personality, his habits and beliefs. All the little gaps that the fan magazines and newspaper articles had failed to fill, Karen had meticulously covered with material derived from her own needs, her own thoughts, and—first and last—her own immaculate love for Elvis. She spoke of him with infinite belief, as though she had actually met him and was well acquainted with him. She treated him with gentle familiarity and warm affection, the way you would a dear, old friend.

Elvis was a man of goodness and compassion—otherwise why would the good Lord bless him with so much good fortune and prosperity? Karen's logic was innocently naive. There was no room for doubt or hesitation in her mind.

I had accepted her confidence. I had taken her enormous secret into my hands with the mute promise to guard and protect it. Instinctively, I knew that I now had to accept her glorious image of Elvis and make it mine, without question and without any thwarted shadows of hesitation or doubt.

The story about Elvis was copious and endless. I listened and learned. Karen spent her lifetime telling it to me. Yet, it seems that in the end we still ran out of time and that there was so much left unsaid.

There were incidents in his life, little episodes which she had read or heard about and carefully hidden in her heart. There was the incredible development of his career, and the transformation from a simple, country boy into an opulent king. Above all, there was Elvis as a person, a friend.

I started to buy magazines for Karen that were devoted to exclusive admiration for Elvis. I bought her pictures, photographs and newspaper cuttings. I bought his records and increased Karen's precious collection until it was perfect and complete.

As time passed, I was constantly confounded by the immeasurable importance Elvis had in Karen's life. In the midst of the listless gray of hopelessness and despair that colored her existence, Elvis's presence sparkled like a piece of priceless jewelry. He filled her thoughts. He occupied her dreams. It seemed that, somehow, by his mere existence, he brought happiness and fulfillment into her life.

Responsibility was a heavy burden on my shoulders. Karen's confident faith in Elvis made my own frail doubt seem painfully obvious. I kept asking myself whether I was doing the right thing. Perhaps I was leading her astray, into unrealistic hopes and expectations. Maybe it would be more honest to bring her back to reality? Should I show her how false and ludicrous her love for Elvis might look in the eyes of this cruel world? Should I shatter her dreams of Elvis? Would a quick, clean wound now hurt less than increasing disappointment in the future?

But I did not have the strength required for that kind of reality. I could not kill the only thing that apparently ever really mattered in Karen's life. All I had to do was look at Elvis's mournful eyes and listen to the joy and happiness in Karen's voice as she spoke of him, and I knew that I would continue to preserve her illusions about his godlike perfection.

Time hurried on in its dependable manner. We woke up one morning and found to our delightful surprise that nature had once again performed the miracle of a new season. Winter had been banished. The soft hope of spring smiled everywhere.

Karen and I hurried to escape the early morning drowsiness of the Brown House. We left duties and chores behind in our eagerness to taste the first, sweet freshness of the new season.

The ground was covered by a bashful blue carpet of budding flowers. I picked some with careful gentleness and formed them into a graceful little bouquet in Karen's rigid hands. Her eyes regarded them thoughtfully, and suddenly she spoke with wishful longing in her voice.

"I wonder what *he* is doing right now."

Surprised, I stopped to look at her. Her face was glowing with subtle beauty. Her complexion was smooth and unnaturally pale, with gentle, violet shadows. Her eyes were two, large black jewels, sparkling and enticing with almost hypnotic power, and drawing attention away from the horrifying deformity of her frail body. Her lips shivered slightly. I wondered if it was from emotion or just the constant, spastic tremors roaming about in her face.

True to my established habit of stumbling across solutions and following impulses, I said without thinking:

"Karen, let's see if we can find out. Let's write a letter and ask him!"

She did not answer me with words. No words were necessary. She just stretched her arms silently toward me and pressed her face hard against my shoulder. Her hands jerked pitifully, and my careful little bouquet fell apart and scattered across the ground.

We were ready to compose The Letter.

An invitingly crisp sheet of paper lay between us. We had collected an unnecessarily large supply of pens and pencils and we had carefully posted a Do Not Disturb sign outside the door. The stage was set for action.

Karen's eyes sparkled with expectation. Suddenly a new factor had been introduced into the dream about Elvis. A more concrete possibility. A "maybe."

I could see her thoughts already rushing ahead into the prosperous future. She indulged in an intoxicating fantasy. She described the way Elvis would look when he received her letter. Breathlessly, she told me what his feelings would be when he read it and discovered that it was different and very special compared to the rest of his mail. Her face glowed as she described the way he would almost immediately sit down and write her an endlessly long reply.

With playful curiosity she wondered whether he, too,

would remember our own precaution of hanging a Do Not Disturb sign on the door before he sat down to his precious chore. She worried a little, but it was a sweet, pleasant worry.

Suddenly I was overwhelmed by the cruelty and injustice of life.

Reality stood there, invincible and scornful. I saw our letter lost in a gigantic pile of similar letters from every corner of the world. I saw weeks and months pass before a well-groomed secretary finally reached our humble envelope. I saw her give it a brief, casual glance before she wearily placed it in another pile of mail, even larger than the first one, where it would finally disappear forever.

That was where my fantasy ended and left me with a bitter taste of regret. But Karen chattered eagerly and had no time to notice that my smile had turned bleak and false.

What could I do but continue on the dangerous road I had begun and carry my pitiful task to its dead end? I cursed my own youthful inclination to follow every impulse that entered my mind.

We wrote our letter at last.

It was brief and polite, and far more restrained than our hearts wanted it to be. But, putting it in Karen's words, "We must remember that, after all, he does not know us very well yet."

A little later we walked down the winding road through the lazy stillness of the afternoon and saw our letter solemnly disappear into the hungry stomach of the mailbox. Karen was unusually cheerful and talkative. She diligently figured out how many days it would take for our letter to reach Elvis, how long before he would have the time and opportunity to read it, and when he would finally answer.

"But," I said, succumbing at last to my own miserable doubts. "What if we don't get an answer?"

"Why?"

Karen looked genuinely puzzled. This grim thought had apparently never entered her mind. I could not avoid a sad smile. With a child's innocence and unquestioned belief, her thoughts had followed a straight, clear-cut line of reasoning. We had written a letter to Elvis. The natural consequence of a letter is a reply. So simple. So logical.

"But what if he is just too busy?" I insisted.

Karen looked thoughtful.

"Nobody knows better than you, I am sure, how hard he works, making movies, cutting records—"

"Sure," Karen said confidently. "Of course, he is busy. I know that it may take a while. But, you see, once he reads my letter he will *know*."

"Well, let's hope so. But just in case, would you be very disappointed if you don't hear from him?"

"You worry too much," Karen said with reassurance. "He will answer. You will see."

Karen's faith in Elvis was absolute and limitless. Her conviction that he would answer her letter was unyielding. For me, there were many painful moments when I envied her belief and wished that I could share a tiny morsel of it.

I was in a difficult situation. My own pessimistic doubt was sometimes as great as Karen's gleeful anticipation. With painful wisdom I knew that never before in my life had I made a mistake as fatal as the one which had resulted in the letter to Elvis. My guilt and regret were overpowering. I suffered invisible wounds, knowing that I could not blame anybody but myself. I was personally and gravely aware that there is no simple remedy that heals the damage committed to a human heart.

Karen's heart was already scarred and bruised by all the sordid cruelties her life had contained. The dream about Elvis had provided solace, comfort and consolation. I should have left it at that, and left letter writing out of the picture. I suddenly realized that by sending the letter, I had indirectly provided Elvis with a way of hurting Karen, by inaccessibility and silence.

I asked myself over and over whether I would ever learn to look before I put my foot down, instead of carelessly stumbling ahead in a blind confusion of good intentions. I prayed feverishly that the good Lord would overlook and forgive my impulse and my error. I begged him silently to use his almighty power and goodness to bring the forces I had set into motion to a successful conclusion.

I prayed for a miracle.

Spring slowly matured into summer. The countryside surrounding the Brown House seemed to swell with fertility and abundance. The sun was a blazing, metallic disk shining its life force over the earth. Green was the color of nature's new dress. Life was good and we thrived in the warm days and cool nights.

I was drinking in the sun with the greedy thirst that

follows a long, dark winter. Through half-closed eyelids I glanced at Karen who was relieved from her wheelchair and rested like a princess on a bed of pillows, innumerable and protective. She was reading a little book whose humble charm brought a faint smile of remembrance to my lips. I too had once loved and cherished that book: Stevenson's *A Child's Garden of Verses*.

She was a study in concentration. Her lips moved softly and her hands flickered with spastic impatience as she attempted to turn the pages. Her bony, emaciated fingers were clutched in a rigid, clawlike grip around the book. The tendons in her neck were sinewy, white cords under the skin. There was a deep, frowning furrow between her eyebrows and I could see the muscles faintly twitching at the side of her mouth. The sun sparkled playfully across her hair, giving it a halo of light. Suddenly she smiled and looked up.

"The world is so full of a number of things. I'm sure we should all be as happy as kings," she said.

I joined in her smile.

"What was that?" I wondered.

"It is called "Happy Thought." Do you like it?"

"Sure."

"But don't you think it's *good*? I mean, *true*?"

"Of course."

"You know, sometimes you forget that there are actually so many things to be happy about."

"True." I was beginning to get interested.

"Little things. Things that aren't really important. Or, at least, that's what you think sometimes because they don't seem to matter much."

I agreed.

"But actually, they *are* important, and we should re-member to be grateful for them. Don't you think so?"

She pondered over this thought for a moment or two. Then she looked at me thoughtfully for support and ap-proval. Her solemn reasoning touched me and I wanted to smile, but her seriousness was too great.

"Don't you think?" she repeated questioningly.

"Oh, sure. I agree with you. People get spoiled, I guess, and we forget. We start taking things for granted. We neither see nor think about them any more, let alone appreciate them. The sad thing is that this is something that happens to everybody, even you and me. You know how it is. We get so involved in various things that we never really stop and notice all the little things that we should be happy about."

"Until this poem reminds us," Karen said.

Her statement sounded final. Nothing more was added. We drifted back into the listless silence of the after-noon.

My mind went back to that miserable time that stretched like a dreary, gray carpet through the previous fall, when I was still trying to make contact with Karen. If some-body had told me then that the day would come when I would hear her solemnly speaking of happiness and grateful-ness, I would have laughed scornfully at the preposterous idea. Still, it was less than a year ago. She had come a long way. I praised Elvis. I knew that the credit was his.

Karen was a child of deep seriousness. She carried burdens on her frail shoulders that most of us never even remotely need to approach. Her possibilities for happiness were slim and her limitations endless and destructive. But it seemed to me now that the scars of bitterness that life had given her were slowly turning into humility and the bruises she had received no longer caused hostility but rather grateful acceptance of whatever happiness she was offered.

Deprived of the privilege of leading a full and active life, she had reached out for somebody to take her place as a substitute in life's arena. She had put all her faith in a person who was both willing and able to accept life with all the joyful readiness it deserves. For what was Elvis if not a symbol of life itself? With his explosive singing and exaggerated body movements, he was an ambassador preaching that life was sweet and good. He tempted us to follow his example and grasp every last morsel of enjoyment life had to offer.

Was this the innermost reason for his presence in Karen's life?

What were his feelings, I wondered, for the crowds that came to see him? What were his thoughts when he was alone and brooding? He too must have his moments of question and doubt. After all, even the greatest of men is still just another human being with the same set of feelings and emotions with which we have all been equipped. Did he shrug wearily at all the eager hands and shrill voices that reached for him in an ecstasy, as toward a god? Or did he realize their importance and their frightening power to love or to kill in the flash of an instant? Did he ever, I asked myself, ponder over the life story that lay behind each letter that reached him?

I looked at Karen who had abandoned her book and slept peacefully among her pillows. The sun threw its pitiless light over her features, revealing the delicate fragility of her face. Her cheeks looked hollow and the shadows under her eyes were a dark violet. Even in her sleep, her eye-lids fluttered restlessly and her facial muscles would occasionally twitch. Her body was like that of a concentration camp prisoner, ravaged with illness and neglect. Her legs were nothing but the bony outline of a skeleton, covered with drab, white skin, and her feet fell in an unnatural angle inwards, brutally revealing the extent of her handicap. She was smiling, tenderly, into the sun.

Right then I suddenly knew that somehow I had to reach Elvis. I wanted to take him by the hand and point to Karen, sleeping in the sun. I wanted to tell him the story about the girl that nobody wanted, the girl life so callously overlooked. I wanted to show him the depths of cruelty and pain she had been subjected to, and also the innocent love he had made her feel. I wanted to say to him, "Thank you for putting that smile on her lips. Thank you for letting her, just once in her life, know what happiness is." In my heart I knew that if Elvis despite the declarations of the crowds that he was a god and a king, was still a human being, then the story about Karen had to mean something to him.

"Dear God," I prayed, "please have Elvis answer Karen."

We proceeded on the gloomy road of waiting. At first, every morning carried with it a new ray of light and hope. Karen's faith was strong and unyielding and her insistence that we would get a reply from Elvis would sometimes tempt even me to believe that my prayers would be fruitful after all.

When one month had gone by without a letter, our disappointment grew. The determined sparkle of hope in Karen's eyes was beginning to fade and was replaced by a weary look of forlorn bewilderment. My own heart felt like a painful lump in my chest, aching with regret and helplessness. What could I do? My sin had already been committed and my guilt tortured me day and night.

We could no longer escape the inevitable. We had no choice but to face the truth in all its ugliness! Elvis was not going to reply to our letter.

By now I knew what I had quietly suspected for a long time and yet, somehow, had stubbornly refused to believe. Somebody else had said it long before me. There is no such thing as a miracle.

"I don't understand—" Karen said, her eyes dark with worry.

"What is the matter?"

"Something must have happened."

"What are you talking about?" I said, although I knew only too well what was to come. We had reached the point where everything had to be brought out honestly into the open and faced squarely. I knew that it was going to be awkward and painful. It was also inevitable.

"My letter. Something has gone wrong."

"Maybe, Karen. Who knows—"

"It is very far away, isn't it?"

"Sure is."

"And then there are all those people."

"What people?"

"You know. Everybody around him. Secretaries and bodyguards and people, just people."

"Of course."

She thought for a minute.

"You see, I was wondering if perhaps somebody else could have accidentally gotten my letter and read it. A secretary, perhaps. But you see, a secretary would never *understand*!"

"I know, Karen."

"I'm almost sure, because if he had read it himself I know, I just *know*, that he would have answered a long time ago."

"Well, then. What do we do now?"

"I don't know. We'll have to think of something."

I was relieved. The damage was apparently not as severe as I had feared it might be. She seemed more confused and bewildered than hurt. But where do we go from here, I wondered. Where do we go from here?

One morning Karen approached me with a suggestion.

"You know," she said seriously. "I have been thinking and I have come to a conclusion."

"Let's hear it."

"Well, I just thought that if everything else fails, there is still one thing to do. It is just about foolproof."

"What would that be?"

"You will have to go and see him."

I needed several minutes to prepare my answer. All at

once my efficient, practical mind started working. I envisioned enormous expense, weary hours of traveling, passports and visa, and finally the search for Elvis in his own, vast country, and the futile efforts to get an instant of his precious time.

I regarded Karen's sensitive face which looked at me with innocent trust and vulnerable expectation.

"Yes, Karen," I said vaguely. "Maybe. If everything else should fail."

"I knew you would do it," she said quietly.

Summer grew quickly and we were inevitably approaching another good-bye.

We were only a short distance away from the end of the school year and our reward was to be three generous months of freedom and vacation. The children looked pale and tired after the long winter and the breathlessly brief spring. The Brown House seemed to be longing to open up its arms and release its little inhabitants to the nourishing warmth of summer. Once again, they would be leaving. Not only for one meager week this time, but for the incredible eternity of a whole, long summer. Once again there would be leisure, laziness and an abundance of time.

Karen regarded the growing anticipation of the Brown House with numb resignation. Nine summers had come and gone and they all looked the same. Quiet, uneventful, boring. Karen was a lifetime prisoner in the Brown House. Even during the summer holidays, she remained in the infinite loneliness that was left behind after the rest of the children had spread their wings and flown off into the blissful land of summer vacation.

As summer came closer, it seemed brutal and callous to exclude any child from the sweet pleasures and spicy freedom of a summer vacation. As it turned out, this time Karen was the only one without a place to go. This struck me as yet another act of sheer, pure cruelty.

And since destiny seldom lends its ear to human complaints, I saw no other way but to finally take the matter into my own hands and try to create justice where fate so obviously had made a brutal oversight.

As time went by, an idea slowly began to take shape within me. I did some quick figuring, trying to consider every practical difficulty that I might possibly run into. One morning I walked into the headmistress's office with my head erect and my little speech prepared for presentation. But my worries were unnecessary and the objections I had anticipated were only mild and easy to overcome. The headmistress smiled at me with knowledge and understanding as I anxiously confronted her with my plan.

"My child," she said with that mild, motherly quality which always made me think of a nun or a saint. "This is against every rule and regulation, as you very well know."

She paused briefly and smiled gently at me before she continued.

"I would not give you my permission, were it not for that poor child. But then, no law is ever so important that it should not from time to time be overlooked and disregarded. There are moments, like now, when even the most fundamental regulation must be pushed aside in order to bring happiness to a child in pain."

The headmistress was a saintly woman who could not let anybody down.

And so, as the children in the Brown House eagerly counted each day to summer, the decision was quietly made and the plans carefully worked out. Except for the headmistress, it was my very own secret. I luxuriated in the warm comfort it gave.

And then, one morning the children left, gone to their summer friends and carefree pleasures.

They took life and laughter with them as they wheeled, hopped, or were carried out the door. Gone was the steady beat of crutches and the moaning squeaks of wheelchairs. The life force itself was gone from the rambling old Brown House.

Summer stood fertile and smiling outside the door, waiting for them with all its yet untasted sweetness. Little cheeks blossomed and little voices danced through the air as they rushed to meet the thrills of this new freedom. With childish impatience they had no time for tender good-byes, and the house that had so carefully sheltered them during the long winter was already forgotten. Suddenly the Brown House looked old and weary. It seemed to fall apart in the vast measure of silence and emptiness. The classrooms were deserted and listless. The chairs in the dining room were neatly stacked in orderly piles of threes and fours. The broad staircase reached in silence for the second floor, its steps suddenly showing cracks and scratches.

The Brown House had no purpose or function in the

summer. It was really a winter house. That was the season when it offered a warm embrace of life and friendliness. That was when it waited with its crackling fireplaces and hot cups of coffee and chocolate like a warm haven or cozy roadside inn in the countryside. Without the children, the Brown House seemed to have lost its reason to exist.

Karen was sitting on the patio, pretending to enjoy the sun.

"Gee, it's quiet," I said cheerfully.

"Uh-huh."

"So we are alone again. Three months of summer ahead of us. Imagine!"

"Yeah."

"What are we going to do with so much time? Have you given it a ′ thought?"

She did not answer. I could sense that she found me annoying.

"I don't care," she finally said.

The moment had come at last when my secret had to be brought out into the open. I smiled to myself.

"Look, Karen," I said. "We have things to do and I need your help. I have a brand new suitcase for you and a cab is picking us up in half an hour so we will have to pack in a hurry."

Karen looked at me in disbelief. Her hands started fluttering and her face got pale and tense. After several minutes of silence, and with tremendous difficulty, she finally managed to speak.

"But how—where are we going?"

Her voice trembled with emotion: fear, joy, confusion.

"You know, I wish that I could have taken you somewhere special, but my place will have to do. At least you won't be spending your vacation all alone in this place all summer. Well, how about it? Do you think you would like to come with me?"

The emotion was just too much for her to control. Tears welled up in her eyes. Her lips moved in a desperate attempt to speak but somehow her muscles were paralyzed by the effort and no sound was heard. Gently, I put my arms around her rigid, trembling body and held her until the seizure slowly died out.

The packing was done in a hurry, for Karen's belongings were humble and few. At last she pointed silently to the little nightstand. No words were needed. We both knew.

I very carefully placed the records and the pictures on top of everything else in the suitcase. Elvis smiled at me as I closed the lid.

The last we saw of the Brown House was the headmistress who stood on the front porch as we slowly rolled down the driveway. She looked very serious and her eyes were filled with something that resembled sorrow.

We were rocking gently in the backseat of the cab, traveling through a countryside that was dressed in summer splendor. The trees were cloaked in frilly, green dresses, clustered together in threes and fours like groups of shy schoolgirls. The sky was a vast sea of blue above us and the air was spiced with all the sweet fragrances of summer. Karen received a friendly reception from the outside world on her first visit away from the Brown House.

I held her tightly pressed against me, trying to infuse her with a feeling of comfort and security. Her body was rigid and cramped in an awkward position now that she was without the dependable support of the wheelchair. Her muscles quivered and jerked under the strain but she did not seem to be aware of it. Her eyes feasted on the passing scenery. They devoured the earth that lay in rich, black furrows in the fields. They tasted the fragrant, whispering forest where, every now and then, a friendly little house peeked out between the tree trunks, as if curious to see us pass by. They lingered greedily on the winding road that we left like a dusty, velvety ribbon behind us.

An absentminded little smile played on her lips. "So this is the world," she seemed to be thinking. "So this is the real, outside world." There was relief in her eyes. The "real" world did not look so strange or unfriendly as she may have feared.

Karen was a child of hopes and dreams, but she also had an instinctive knowledge of truth and reality which guided her thoughts and reasoning. She knew that, in spite of its tempting beauty, the outside world was not for her. It would never be, except perhaps for some moments of borrowed time.

Still, suddenly destiny had become surprisingly generous. Karen had been permitted to take a step into the real world. She had a "visitor's pass" for three long months. For three months she would be in the midst of the world, and a living, breathing part of it. I felt her rigid body shivering in my arms. As I looked down, I noticed tears running down her cheeks.

The road made one final loop over a hilltop and then

the city lay spread out before our eyes like an exquisite piece of jewelry. Beyond the city was the ocean, infinite in its blue splendor. The sun glinted on the water that seemed to curve in soft ringlets around the islands that made up the city. The whole world seemed suspended in time, resting in a moment of peace and tranquility.

Wordlessly, I wiped Karen's tear-stained cheek. Happiness is seen at its most intense when you see it mirrored in a child's face. Karen's joy at that moment was close to a kind of ecstasy of the spirit, one that she had never known before and would never know again.

That evening we sat by the window, watching the city come to rest. Dusk crept swiftly across the rooftops and descended to the streets. It embraced the city in a smoky blue veil that silently deepened and turned to purple. The air was still, trembling with expectation. The traffic noise sounded like a hollow echo from another world. For one breathless moment time seemed to hesitate, as though overwhelmed by the transition from day to night.

The day was over and the city was catching its breath to gain strength for the activities of the approaching night.

The stereo played softly behind us. Elvis's voice rose and sank on waves of tenderness, as if he had seen our pensive peacefulness and did not want to shatter it. He sang romantic songs as if he were actually in the room with us, sharing our mood of melancholy and intimacy.

At that moment I could almost feel his presence.

Funny, I said to myself, that I had never before noticed the gentle sadness in his voice. Any person whose voice could express such a quality of calm, of profound sensitivity had to know the full range of feelings and emotions.

I was beginning to understand how Karen felt. I knew why he was the great man in her life. Why, indeed, it *had* to be him, and nobody else.

Perhaps it was just a trick played by the sheer summer evening. Perhaps it was Karen's love that finally had managed to persuade me. Or perhaps it was really Elvis himself who had finally succeeded in touching me. I shall never know for sure. But I suddenly realized that Elvis had entered our lives for a reason. He had come to bring happiness. He would not let us down. I knew it as surely as if he, himself, had told me. No longer because of Karen. No longer because I was forced to believe it. But because I was finally convinced.

He had come suddenly and unannounced into her life. They had met—Elvis Presley and the little girl who had nothing to look forward to in life. And as long as Elvis lived in her heart, Karen would live too. And, most importantly, she would be happy.

He ought to know, I thought, that just by existing, without even being aware of it, he has performed a miracle. He has given strength and hope to another human being. He has given a reason and an incentive to live to a helpless child who had found no happiness in life.

Karen also was lost in thought. My friendly Siamese cat snuggled affectionately on her lap and Karen's stiff fingers traveled in awkward stroking movements across its silky fur. Her eyes rested pensively on the intense purple of the night sky.

"Karen," I said softly, reluctant to spoil her moment of thoughtfulness. "What are you thinking about?"

She did not answer.

"Were you thinking about him?"

She nodded slowly.

"What are your thoughts when you think about him?"

She groped for an answer. The seriousness in her face was great. At last, her voice came soft and trembling.

"I—I think that—Well, I wonder what he is doing. I wonder what he is thinking. And—and I worry sometimes that—I mean, I wish—I wish—I just like him so very much," she added quietly.

"I know, Karen."

We remained silent for a while. Then it was her turn to speak again.

"You know, sometimes I wonder—"

"What?"

"I wonder what he will write about in his letter."

"Mmmm."

"I wonder if he will tell his friends about me. Maybe he will make a record for me. I mean, one that is meant only for me."

I regarded Karen in silent wonder. Her words lingered in my mind, and I felt envy, awe, and admiration. So great was the measure of her faith in Elvis that it knew no limit and it knew no doubt.

K͟aren eventually succumbed to her fatigue, although reluctant to admit that her first day in the real, normal world had come to an end. She slept peacefully in the comforting knowledge that the morning would bring another day of discovery and adventure.

Her hair floated in ringlets over the pillow, like an exquisite fan made out of precious silk. Her eyelids were shadowed by a thin streak of violet, barely visible above the dark fringe of lashes. Her breathing came in long, regular intervals, enhancing the stillness of the night and evoking in my heart a feeling of eternal loneliness.

Her hand lay trustingly in mine, only occasionally moved by a slight flutter. A smile played tenderly across her lips, giving her face a quality of mysterious beauty. For a moment I wondered what she was dreaming about and then I knew. Only one person could ever bring that softness to her face. Elvis.

In this time of sleep and dreams he is very much real and alive to her, and nothing is impossible for her any longer.

Karen's thin face lay against the pillow. Her eyes were nothing but dark shadows in the faint light of the summer night. Her body was outlined with feathery light contours under the covers. She was so frail. So fragile.

It was at moments like this that I discovered the beauty that life had given her. It was not physical perfection or classic regularity. It was the beauty of innocence and compassion, the purity of an angel.

I buried my face in my hands, clasping my fingers in desperate prayer, and opening them up again.

My will was so strong, but my helplessness was greater. I was only nineteen years old and so far in my life I had obediently followed the roads destiny had pointed out to me, never asking where they ultimately would lead. I had never pursued a great star before, nor had I thought about how you found a way that would reach him. I did not know how that sort of thing was done.

"God, why did you not give me the power to perform a miracle? One. Just one. Not for myself, but for Karen."

The night was deaf to my prayers. Gently, I loosened my grip around Karen's hand and found my way back into the living room. The whole world was asleep around me as I sat down to write Karen's story to Elvis. A story about the girl that nobody wanted who had a glorious dream. The story was about Elvis and for Elvis.

I wrote slowly and with all the seriousness my heart contained. I wrote of the cruelty, the pain, the evil. I wrote of faith, gratitude, and love. I wrote of weakness and helplessness, of despair and suffering, of waiting and praying for a miracle. Every word was born out of the gloomy pain in my heart. Every sentence was created out of the dark misery in my soul.

The letter was a plea, a prayer, a shrill cry for help from one human being to another.

As the first rays of dawn emerged at the horizon, I finally put down my pen. I was tired. My letter to Elvis was finished. The story of Karen was in front of me in all its ugly reality, set down in my own handwriting. There was nothing more to add.

The last traces of night rose on silvery wings, once again making room for morning. I turned on the phonograph and listened to Elvis's gentle voice. His face on the record cover looked longingly and mysteriously into mine. At that moment I felt lonelier and more helpless than ever. Tears of anguish and fatigue ran down my cheeks. I knew that what we really needed was nothing short of a miracle.

Elvis sang on, his voice full of tenderness, full of compassion. As if he had seen. As if he had known. . . .

Despite its usual independent manner, there are moments when destiny seems to consider our human wishes and obey them. Suddenly one morning, destiny decided to indulge in this kind of benevolence.

We were still at the breakfast table making plans for the day when we were interrupted by the telephone. It was a dear old friend, an artist, who had only one day left in town before he turned his steps toward white, palm-shaded beaches and clear, blue waters. Would I help him fill his thirst for the Scandinavian summer this last day before he left? His ancient car was still dependable enough to carry us far into the untouched freshness of the countryside. I could not resist his friendly invitation, provided, of course, that I could bring a little girl along. His bubbling laughter in the receiver confirmed our deal.

And so our conversation was over long before I ever got a chance to tell him more about the child he was going to meet. I did not get a chance to warn him not to be frightened, not to react too obviously, not to talk too much or joke too often, not to laugh too loud so that she got frightened. . . .

"We'll have to hurry up with our breakfast," I said as matter-of-factly as I could. "We're going to have a visitor. Maybe we'll go to the country."

I saw the sudden twitch in her face and the look of uneasy apprehension in her eyes. Being alone with me was one thing. I had been tested and somehow found acceptable, despite my numerous failings. In the company of strangers, though, Karen always closed her petals in scared shyness.

Mingled with my tender wish to protect this little child from any unnecessary stress was a strong feeling of wanting to push her ahead into new situations. I wanted her to try, to dare, and to give life another chance. I wanted Karen to come out of her shell and meet the world, to discover that it could be, at times, a safe and friendly place to be. There were times, like now, when I even thought it necessary to leave her without a choice. Yet, for a moment I was chilled by fear. But then, I had not counted on the artist himself.

He waddled through the door with the majestic contentment of a rugged old bear quietly humming to himself as he munches berries in the sun. His beard grew happily in all directions. His clothes were spotted with paint. Somewhere, under bushy eyebrows, his eyes glistened small and penetratingly blue with wisdom and laughter. His smile was broad and generous and somewhere from out of his baggy pockets, he pulled a large box of candy.

He was Santa Claus in the middle of summer.

Karen was astounded. She was trapped by his unusual charm long before her instinctive hostility ever got a chance to awaken. I could see the hesitation disappear from her eyes and be replaced by a bewildered sympathy and admiration for this funny character. She had never met anybody like this before. She did not even know that people like the artist existed.

Meeting a "different" child generally presents an awkward situation for most people. We are either too cautious and considerate or falsely "natural" about the situation. Most of us are too uncomfortable and too embarrassed to remain honest and normal. Not so the artist. He knew instinctively what to do. He never pretended that he did not see or that he was not aware. He made it clear that he realized Karen's situation, but also, most importantly, that he really could not care less.

His laughter roared through the apartment and the jokes fell like pearls from his lips. His bubbling personality seemed to reach Karen. She sensed the sincerity beneath this cheerful surface. With her deep feeling for honesty, she knew that this individual was real, and a person who could safely be trusted.

She was quiet as usual, neither moving nor talking. But her eyes glistened and every so often she would laugh. She was surprised and impressed.

"This is good for you, Karen," I thought. "This is one side of the human race which you never knew anything about. Today you are going to learn a lot."

The sun was blazing and the air heavy and hot. The dust formed a thick, gray cloud behind us as we guided the car through the prosperous summer country. The flowers stretched and turned their faces toward the sun and birds floated gingerly in the vast, blue endlessness above.

Karen drank the summer in thirsty gulps. Her hair was streaming in the air. She laughed as the car hobbled across bumpy roads and clutched my hand as the artist kept pouring his jokes over us. The world was suddenly at her feet. Nature was squandering its beauty in front of her and the sun tempted some freckles to appear on her nose. She was alive, alive to everything around her.

My heart was full of happiness and sadness. Somewhere in the back of my mind was the inevitable image of the Brown House. I feared the day when it would call us back.

The artist's arms were strong and secure. Confidently, they carried Karen across fields and meadows. They rolled her through the grass and held her in the serene stillness of the forest. He showed Karen how to run her fingers over the roughness of a tree trunk. He splashed her feet in a silvery brook. Together they lay in the grass watching ladybugs climb swiftly between the leaves. Then they turned around and laughed at the cotton-ball clouds drifting across the sky. Karen touched, smelled, listened, and laughed. For one lovely summer day the world was hers.

But time crept in on us. Only too soon the first evening breeze was whispering through the trees.

Happily exhausted, we turned back to the city. The smell of the sun was still in our hair and the sweet taste of freedom was still on our lips. Karen sat silently in my lap, with rosy cheeks and laughter still in her eyes. She had never had a happier day.

The breath of the city was hot and slow. Gingerly, the evening sent a soft breeze over the sidewalks like a soothing hand on a feverish cheek. Our adventure was just about over. There was only one thing remaining.

"My princess shall have a present!" laughed the artist. "A farewell gift, in memory of this day."

He disappeared into a drugstore and returned with a square package in brown paper. His blue eyes sparkled with friendliness as he hugged Karen good-bye. Then he was suddenly gone, along with his forceful laughter and incessant jokes. Suddenly the evening seemed empty and silent.

Karen fumbled with the package. The paper finally fell aside. We were both eager to see what he had bought.

Karen froze in surprise. For an instant she remained motionless, breathless. And then, as if exhaustion had caught up with her at last, she fell apart. She buried her hands in her stiff fingers and cried long, desperate sobs.

A chill ran down my spine. Completely mystified, I stared at Karen and the present the artist had given her. Had he known? Had he guessed? Was it all coincidence or an act of God? We would never know for sure.

The gift he gave Karen was an Elvis Presley record.

I still remember the first thought that entered my mind as soon as my shock was over. Could this be the miracle that I had prayed for? Was it God's indirect way of spelling out the words *Keep on!*?

Once more we faced the task of writing to Elvis. The blue piece of paper lay crisp and smooth in front of us. Pale blue. I thought of sadness, loneliness.

"Not again," I whispered to myself. "No, once is enough. This time we'll reach him. This time he'll answer."

And I *wanted* to believe it. But disappointment is so dangerous, so contagious that it leaves no room for hope. It has no pity, not even for a child.

Karen was too busy with her letter to Elvis to notice my despair. Her hair fell down over her forehead as she strained to print letter after letter in an uneven line across the paper. Concentrating. Unaware. Innocent. Confident.

Karen's hands were traveling in stubborn determination back and forth across the paper. Her fingers were clasped in a tight, rigid grip around the pen. Every now and then a quick, involuntary jerk would fling the pen out of her hand, and each time it was followed by the long, pitiful procedure of retrieving it again. Very slowly the words grew across the paper. Crooked and trembling they danced in uneven lines against the blue background.

Her whole body was a bundle of straining muscles and raw nerves. I could see the arteries on the side of her neck, pulsating under the skin. I saw the thin, quivering lines around her mouth. I knew that her back was tense with pain. I knew that I should speak up and tell her that she must not . . . It was my responsibility as her protector and friend. She was not aware of it herself right then, but later on she would have to pay the price for this enormous effort.

But I did not speak. I kept all my sensible words to myself. Some moments must be silent.

How strange, I thought gloomily, that the two of us were sitting there, so close and yet so different. My body was perfect, Karen's was not. I had a future, and she did not. Yet, Karen was the one who had faith where I did not. She was the one who gave me hope and reassurance when I needed it the most. She calmed my inner turmoil with her confidence and belief.

Nature had given her a body which was painfully defective. Life had threatened to drown her in loneliness and sorrow. Society had turned its back on her in contempt and disgust. Still, she sat there, totally unperturbed, lost in her glorious dream about Elvis.

While my mind carried me across these dark pathways, Karen kept on writing. Awkwardly, her fingers guided the pen through obstacles of pain and fatigue. The words danced in wild loops and ringlets like funny, crippled, little birds rising and falling in the distant blue of a happy summer sky.

Every evening we would sit by the open window, watching the city in front of us. We both loved that translucent moment of infinite peace when night arrived slowly, stealthily. Invariably, Elvis would be singing in the darkness behind us. His voice would be the only one heard. Gently. Tenderly.

One night Karen suddenly broke our unwritten rule of silence.

"This is so beautiful," she whispered dreamily. I was not sure if her words were directed to me or if she had suddenly given voice to her thoughts.

And suddenly I knew that someday there would be moments just as beautiful as this, which I would know in loneliness, without Karen by my side. Moments which would be filled with remembrance and pain.

It was like knowing that a great sadness has already been prepared for you. I knew that I already had been given much more than I ever could have asked for. God had given me the miracle of Karen, the infinite gift of knowing and loving his child. But even a miracle cannot last forever. It must come to an end and say good-bye. I realized that when the time was up I would have no choice. I would have to part from Karen, thankful for what we had shared, realizing that there never again would be anyone like her to grace my life.

A line of poetry suddenly came to mind. "Even if there will be no tomorrow, the birds sing today."

Overcome by emotion, I reached out into the darkness, grasping for Karen who regarded me in astonishment. I embraced her so tightly that she moaned in pain, but I would not let her go. I rocked her in my arms. Our cheeks were side by side and our tears mingled together as they fell from our eyes.

Summer slipped softly by. Karen and I created memories together like a sparkling string of pearls, one after another.

One night we went to a movie. So unimportant. So meaningless. But no! Not for us.

The evening breeze caressed our faces with warm, gentle fingers. The twilight painted the world in sheer, violet pastels. Somewhere in the remote distance echoed a signal from a ship at sea. Sad. Moaning. Longing.

Karen had never been to a movie theater before. That night I experienced the excitement of going to a movie for the first time all over again. The pleasant taste of adventure and the sweet smell of expectation. The lights. The laughing, chattering crowds. That wonderful feeling of something just about to happen.

Karen's eyes were bottomless wells of turbulence and delight. At the same time, she was scared beyond belief.

Her thin little hand was clutching mine in desperation and excitement. The theater was a stormy ocean of human beings. A thrilling spectacle of mirrors and red velvet and the aromas of cigarette smoke, perfume, and warm human bodies. I looked at Karen and she seemed to be the littlest person in the world. She looked so out of place in this setting of artificial sophistication. Yet, a very special purpose had brought her here tonight. Unlike the rest of the audience, she had not come for entertainment, relaxation, amusement, or escape. Karen's reason for being there was much simpler, and much more important. She had come to meet, for the first time in her life, her oldest and dearest friend. She had come to see Elvis.

Her hand lay trembling in mine. Her cheeks were two feverish red roses. Her eyes flew rapidly back and forth between the audience and the white screen in front of us.

She loved him. She knew every tone of his voice, every line in his face, with the familiarity that inevitably grows out of love. She must have seen every picture and photograph of him that had ever been published. But never had she seen him move or speak or sing. Never had she seen his face light up in a smile. Tonight he would come alive for her.

After an eternity of waiting, the lights finally dimmed, softly and drowsily. The huge curtains parted with solemn dignity, in preparation for this awesome meeting.

And in a moment Elvis, many times larger than life, appeared on the screen. Karen sat enchanted at his every gesture.

The movie was over. Once again we were back in the real world. But there was still the faintest trace of unreality lingering around us.

We were, of course, talking about Elvis.

"You see, it was all so true," Karen smiled into the darkness as she lay in her bed, unable to sleep.

"How do you mean?"

"Everything that I knew about him. It was just the way that I thought it would be."

"You mean—"

"You know, the way he walks and talks. That sort of thing."

"Mmmm. I see."

"I knew it already, you see. I just *knew* it."

She thought about it for a minute. Then she added: "Isn't that strange?"

"What?"

"Isn't it strange that even though I had never seen him in person before, I knew what he was like."

"Yes, that is strange."

"But that isn't all. There is more. I know even more about him. You know, things that I have never heard or read, and yet I know it just as well as if somebody had told me. Just as if we were really friends."

"Well, you are. Sort of."

"But I mean as if we had met and talked several times."

Her voice sounded strong and jubilant. For a moment my heart shivered with love and wonder. I was grateful for the shadows that concealed my face.

"And do you know the strangest thing of all?"

Karen continued. "I know that someday I will reach him and I will get to know him really well. We'll be friends, just like you and me. I know it, don't you see? I just *know* it."

Summer was fading away. It had come and now it was going, the way summers will always come and go. The only difference was that this was the only summer that ever really mattered.

The Brown House was calling us again.

It stood there, dignified and majestic among the trees, just the way we had left it. Once again it embraced us with its noisy friendliness and our lives changed from freedom to schedule and routine.

And we said nothing, for that was the way it had to be.

Autumn came subtly, with chilly, translucent mornings and frostbitten grass. Quietly we watched the birds fly south across the fading blue sky. Nature exploded in a splendor of red and gold, like a final burst of laughter before the silence of the imminent winter.

Karen's freedom was once again limited to our strolls through the forest. Our little road curled like a brown, velvet ribbon between the solemn pines. A squirrel jumped swiftly among the branches and some leaves rustled gracefully to the ground.

"Why do they fall off?" Karen wondered.

"Because the time has come for them to fall off and die."

"What a pity!"

"Well, it's really just nature's way, you know. They

have to fall off in order to leave room for new leaves next spring."

"Yes, but it seems so cruel, that they should die right now when everything is so colorful and pretty."

"Well, try to look at it this way, Karen. If they die when the earth is still at its peak of beauty, then they will never have to suffer the cold and misery that comes with winter."

She smiled. The thought seemed to please her.

It is strange to love somebody who lives close to death. It is like reaching for a shadow which escapes between your fingers, or like picking a budding flower, knowing that the moment you break its tender stalk, it will begin to wither.

Autumn grew in size and shape. The air seemed gloomy and thin. Each new morning arose with a veil of mist draped around its shoulders.

We spent our days writing letters to Elvis and waiting for his answer. But he did not seem to hear us calling him and he did not reply.

And so, while gloominess grew more oppressed outside the window, a little bit of it seemed to find its way inside. And as autumn turned soggy and gray, once again I was overcome by desperation.

There are moments when I am overcome by an irresistible desire to be alone. To vanish into nothingness. Those are the times when I truly enjoy walking in the crowds of a busy street, devoured by its anonymity. That is when I hurry to shut my windows and lock my door and indulge in the peace of solitude and the sound of silence.

The longing for this kind of loneliness overcame me one morning as I was on my way to the Brown House. Karen was waiting. I experienced a sensation of guilt and relief as I saw the train leaving without me, knowing that there would not be another one along for a full hour. One hour of being alone. That was all I asked for.

The air felt cold against my face. It filled my heart with a chill of powerlessness, of hopelessness.

The look of confidence in Karen's eyes was dying and the cheerfulness in her voice was fading. I had already seen the first, unmistakable signs of letdown and disappointment. Pain was beginning to seek its way back into her movements. Her thoughts about Elvis were no longer fiery with faith and reassurance, but had started to flicker in doubting anguish. Elvis seemed remote, distant, more and more a dream, less and less a reality.

Karen was not asking for much. Just a sign from Elvis that, somehow, he cared.

We had reached a point where everything seemed to come to a halt. Seven months had passed since she first introduced me to Elvis. Seven months of writing letters and waiting for his reply.

Surely, there were those who waited for years, without disruption in either faith or devotion? But they were the strong ones, the healthy ones, those who could afford to wait. Without her dream, Karen would be nothing. If she lost Elvis she would also lose her reason for clinging to life. For, although the professionals did not know the proper name of the force that so miraculously kept Karen alive, there was no doubt that it was Elvis. The doctors, the therapists, the nurses, steeped in medical knowledge and wisdom, had seen their grave predictions shattered to pieces. Against all theory and against all logic, Karen was still alive. Even the headmistress, had commented on the strange power that had transformed Karen and was propelling her forward. I was the only one privileged enough to know about Elvis. Without him, what would be left for Karen? Without Karen, what would be left for me?

I sought refuge from the cold in a little coffee shop while waiting for the next train. I stirred my coffee in endless circles and watched the steam from the cup vanish into the air. I felt young, lonely, scared.

Somebody had left a magazine on the next table. There he was, Elvis, smiling gently at me from a photograph. I was no longer surprised. My strange meetings with Elvis in all places, at all times, had eventually become a habit.

Anyway, I would tear out the picture and bring it to Karen. Perhaps it would cheer her up a little. There was an article, too. "An intimate report from our correspondent in Hollywood who is personally acquainted with Elvis Presley and a close friend of his . . ."

Somewhere in the back of my mind a thought was wearily born. It was nothing but a fleeting idea, colored by fatigue and desperation. I wondered what would happen if I wrote to the Hollywood correspondent who apparently had such close connections with Elvis. Maybe she would be able to give me some advice, I thought. A hint of direction. A new way to try.

It was a slim ray of light in my grim darkness. It was a *maybe* in a world that had been only saying *no*.

And so, one dreary, November night I wrote still another letter.

As I had tucked Karen into her bed in the Brown

House a few hours earlier, she had suddenly reached out for me and embraced me violently. For a long time we had been sitting there with our arms around each other and I knew that, even though no sound came over her lips, she really wanted very much to cry. There was no longer any doubt that disappointment was beginning to haunt her, and her faith, which had once been both strong and immaculate, was now weak and soiled by despair. In the gloomy silence, my helplessness and inadequacy seemed greater than ever before.

I wondered what kind of person I was really writing to. Somehow her title alone, "Hollywood correspondent," was intimidating. It conjured up images of glamour, sophistication and shallow artificiality. What could a Hollywood correspondent possibly know about Brown Houses, a handicapped little girl's secret love, or the importance of reaching Elvis? I did not give her much credit for understanding or compassion. I was certain that her world consisted of nothing but cocktail parties, movie studios, and gossip. Still, she had definitely one, great advantage. She was supposedly a friend of Elvis's. She knew him well enough to write "intimate reports" about his life.

Overpowered by my own helplessness and a strange mixture of envy and anger at my own heartless image of the Hollywood correspondent, I poured all my frustration, all my despair, and all my frightful powerlessness into my letter to her. I painted her an ugly picture of life in an institution. I told her about human lives that never lead anywhere, except in endless circles of boredom and confinement. I vehemently explained to her the necessity of keeping our dreams alive, and the enormous importance of movie stars, pop idols and rock musicians can have in the lives of plain, everyday, common people. Tears started to run down my cheeks as I told her about Karen. I searched furiously for the right words to describe the beautiful, but unrequited, love this little girl had for Elvis. I told her of the merciless circumstances of Karen's life, her innocent faith, and the tortuous road we had traveled in search of Elvis. I explained our need for a miracle, and pleaded for her help.

Once I got started I found it difficult to stop. It was as if my emotional brakes had been released and I was fulfilling some pent-up, inner need to let all my feelings explode on the pages in front of me. Somewhere in my letter, the Hollywood correspondent disappeared from view and I was no longer writing for her but for myself. And as the night slowly grew deeper and the flames in the fireplace died, I whimpered in pain as I relived my time with Karen. As the pages piled up in front of me, I kept wiping the tears from my eyes more and more frequently. On paper, the story about Karen looked even more miserable and her dream about Elvis even more futile than I had ever before realized. At last I pushed the handwritten pages aside and gave in to a sobbing, seven-month-overdue cry.

Several hours later I woke up, shivering cold, on the floor in front of the fireplace. The first morning light was stealing through the windows and it was time to get ready for the Brown House. I quickly gathered the scattered pages together, signed my name at the bottom and stuffed them into an envelope. I did not have the time to look at what I had written. Besides, I knew instinctively that if I had, then the letter would never get mailed. It was too emotional, too revealing, and too personal. Besides, it was rambling. It was not a good letter, not the kind you send to a Hollywood correspondent.

But what difference did it make? She would not understand anyway. At this point, I doubted if anybody would ever understand my pain, and Karen's. Elvis had been our secret joy for seven months. Now he had become our secret tormentor. Even so, we would share it, Karen and I. Somehow.

On my way to the train I put the letter in a mailbox. Quickly, before there was time for second thoughts. Not until I was already on my train did I realize that I had completely forgotten to ask her advice on how to get in touch with Elvis.

During the next few days the weather suddenly took a turn for the worse. The dense clouds took on a menacing appearance and finally burst open in a thundering rainstorm which drenched us for almost a week. Every now and then, lightning cut jagged strips of fire through the night sky over our heads, with a rage so violent that it automatically brought to mind our human frailty as contrasted to God's might.

Karen looked pale and gloomy. She was listless, quiet, withdrawn. For a day or two she had an annoyingly runny nose. Then she developed a temperature and was immediately ordered to bed by the headmistress. Karen did not seem to mind. She seemed relieved to leave the noisy havoc of the playroom and allowed me to wheel her down to the comforting silence of her bedroom.

Without a word being spoken between us, I undressed her and tucked her into bed. Karen turned her face toward the window where the rain was beating fiercely against the glass. Somehow, I felt as if all of a sudden some mighty force had reversed the machinery of time and put me back on square one, and I was still trying to reach Karen. I had an uneasy feeling of apprehension and fear. Her body was still under the blanket. Her face looked translucent and hollow, and only her eyes were alive, burning with anguish. She was staring intently at the rain which dribbled across the window like teardrops trickling down a cheek.

"Karen," I whispered gently. "How are you doing?"

At first she did not seem to hear me. Then, slowly, she turned her head and regarded me solemnly. The sadness I read in her eyes was so formidable that it frightened me.

"Are you okay?" I asked worriedly.

She nodded.

"I'm worried about you. What's the matter?"

"Nothing."

"Could we talk about it?"

"No."

"Are you thinking about—"

"No." She cut me off short.

"Karen, please don't leave me out. I want to share it with you. We can talk about it."

"There's nothing to talk about. Really."

"Are you hurting anywhere?"

"No."

"Please talk to me. Tell me how you feel."

"I'm very tired," Karen said, turning her head once again away from me. "I think I'd like to go to sleep."

Hurt and bewildered, I watched her curl up under the blanket and close her eyes. I knew that our conversation was over, whatever little there was of it. For the first time in almost a year, Karen had shut me out again. I did not understand why. I knew that she was sick. The cold was getting her down. But for some reason that explanation did not satisfy me. There was more to it than that. It was Elvis, the disappointment that he still had not answered, the fear that perhaps he never would, the thought that he did not care. Oh, God, what could I do?

I suddenly felt hatred and disgust for Elvis. Who did he think he was? Had he managed to become so "great" that he no longer had any connections with the rest of the human race? Did he not realize that wearing the crown of a star not only entails fame and admiration, but also obligation and responsibility? Did he not understand that the vast crowds that gave him his name also had the merciless power to withdraw it at a moment's notice? Surely, he must be aware of the important role he played in millions of lives. Karen needed him more than most of them. Her life depended on him. She had given him her innocent love, her trust, and her endless faith. All she asked in return was a small sign that he cared. A postcard. A letter. What was he going to do about it?

A drum roll of thunder exploded across the sky, interrupting my thoughts, and the heavens sent another shattering downpour over the Brown House. Karen appeared to be asleep. She looked so vulnerable, so forlorn.

Desperate to escape my gnawing gloom, I went looking for the headmistress, who always seemed to have an extra portion of compassion and understanding to give to the needy. And I was more than needy—I was impoverished of hope, of faith, of spirit.

The headmistress sat behind the desk in her office, looking thoughtfully at the storm outside the window. I knocked gently at her half-open door and she turned around and greeted me with a warm smile.

"Come in. Come sit down for a while."

I was beginning to feel better already. There was something about the headmistress that was automatically comforting. She did not have to speak. Just being in her motherly presence gave consolation to troubled souls. There was never any doubt in my mind as to why she had been chosen to preside over the children in the Brown House.

"Such weather!" she said and added quickly: "How is Karen?"

"She is asleep."

"Good. It will do her good. She hasn't been looking well lately."

"I know. That's what I wanted to talk to you about."

"You are worried about her?" the headmistress said quietly.

"Yes, I am. Of course, I am. Something is happening with her. Something bad. Something that she won't let me share with her."

I told her briefly about Karen's strangely cool behavior in the bedroom a short while earlier. The headmistress gave me a long, thoughtful look.

"Well," she finally said. "I wouldn't worry too much about it. I don't think it has much to do with you, really. You have managed to establish a relationship with Karen that I never thought possible. Karen needs you. She knows it. She is not going to destroy anything between you two."

"Go ahead, tell her!" an urgent little voice screamed inside me. "Tell her about Elvis. She needs to know. She might even have some suggestions." But I remained quiet, knowing that the guilt of betraying Karen's confidence would be unbearable.

"But there is something," the headmistress continued. "There is definitely something bothering her. I have seen it for some time now. Frankly, I am surprised that you come to me like this. That she hasn't told you—"

"She knows," I said to myself. "I should have realized that she knows."

"You know," she went on. "There is something else involved here, something much deeper. Although you deserve much credit for helping Karen come out of her shell, you wouldn't have succeeded, had it not been for Karen herself. Something inside her. There is a strong force somewhere that has been pushing her ahead this past year. I don't know what to call it. Now, for some reason, it seems to be subsiding."

"Yes, yes," I thought. "You are right, so right. Now, please go on and tell me what will happen next."

She moved some papers around on her desk and appeared to be deep in thought. Then she looked at me seriously.

"You realize that, in all probability, Karen won't be with us that much longer?"

I stirred uncomfortably in my seat. I had come for consolation, not painful reminders. But the headmistress was not finished.

"I know that you don't like to hear it, but you must. You must know it and believe it and you must prepare yourself, because it will happen. Karen does not have the physical requirements for a long life. She has already surprised us by deceiving the medical predictions. But it cannot go on forever. You must face it. Perhaps what we are seeing now is the first, natural step in that direction."

She must have sensed the anguish choking in my throat because she came around the desk and put her arm carefully around my shoulders.

"I know how you feel," she said tenderly. "It hurts terribly to think about it, but you have no choice. For Karen's sake, as well as for you own, you must prepare yourself before it happens."

She wiped the first of many tears from my cheek.

"Now, go somewhere and think about what I have told you. Have a good cry. And then, go and see to Karen and make sure that you take good care of her for whatever time she has left."

Karen slept through most of the next couple of days. I sat in endless loneliness by her bedside, listening to the rain, and confusedly trying to cope with the desolation inside me.

So, it had been said at last. Karen was going to die. It was no longer just a cruel nightmare that attacked me when I was lonely or tired. It was an evil, inevitable fact. Little by little, I was beginning to understand what the headmistress had told me. I had to accept it. Somehow I had to prepare myself.

But how does anyone ever prepare oneself for the tragedy of death? Each time I looked at Karen's sleeping face I tried to imagine what it would be like. And each time I experienced a forceful urge to grab her, shake her, and wake her up. "No!" I wanted to scream. "Not her! Not yet! There is something we have to do first. We are expecting a letter—"

One afternoon I heard the soft rustle of the headmistress in the doorway. She ran her hand over Karen's forehead and smoothed out the blanket with infinite tenderness. Then she reached into her pocket and handed me a carefully folded sheet of paper.

"Read it," she said. "It has helped me. Perhaps it will help you, too."

Then she left as quietly as she came, and I looked at the paper she had given me. It contained the following:

We learn as much from sorrow as from joy, as much from illness as from health, from difficulty as from advantage—and, indeed, perhaps more. Not out of fullness has the human soul always reached its highest but often out of deprivation.

When one learns to live with sorrow, one learns, too, how to find comfort by the way. When one learns to accept difficulty, one also learns how to take stubbornness by the hand and remain on the battlefield.

By the end of the week the rain stopped. Karen seemed better, and my pain had become a dull, moaning ache in the pit of my stomach.

The headmistress decided that it would be wise for Karen to remain in bed until she had recuperated completely. So I sat by her bedside, reading stories, coloring pictures, and talking softly about anything that happened to come into my mind. Elvis was seldom mentioned. Karen was still thoughtful and relatively unresponsive. I felt instinctively that it would be better not to disturb her wounds, at least not just yet. My own disposition was not too cheerful either right then. And so I decided to let some time pass and see what would happen.

And then it arrived. The letter.

I came home late from the Brown House one night and found it in my mailbox. Surprisingly, it was not pastel colored and perfumed as, somehow, I had expected from a Hollywood correspondent. It was a plain, ordinary business envelope where a number of foreign-looking stamps were crowding in the upper-right-hand corner. I stood there with the letter in my hand and knew, numb with fear all of a sudden, that the moment of judgment had arrived. My hands were shaking uncontrollably. Something told me that the verdict would be against us.

Our helplessness was too great. It was insane to reach for a dream. Karen was going to die. She was never going to see her dream come true. She would leave the dreary existence she had been born to without ever tasting the sweet wine of happiness. Life was cruel. Life did not have any compassion. Life ignored unrealistic dreams about great men.

I had the evidence in my hand. I read the words I had expected to see. The Hollywood correspondent was a woman who knew that miracles were only too rare. Her letter was compassionate but apologetic.

Yes, she was indeed acquainted with Elvis. She had met him several times. Polite. Well mannered. Almost shy. Busy, too. Getting a reply from him was next to impossible, of course. Thousands of letters each week. Naturally, one would have to understand. A picture could certainly be arranged. She would see to it. But, beyond that, it would be cruel on her part to get our hopes up. My letter had touched her very much. She could understand, because she had a daughter only a few years younger than Karen. She would try. She would make some phone calls.

But, please do not expect too much. Do write again. . . .

There went the last brittle strands of hope. There died the final attempt at reaching Elvis. It was extinguished as easily as you blow out a burning candle. The dream of reaching Elvis had become a nightmare.

My pain became a fierce scream of anguish. Had I not known all along that it would end just like this? Desperately, I had clung to the hope of a miracle, believing that somehow the good Lord would know how important it was that he help us.

The Hollywood correspondent understood the magnitude of the hopelessness we were facing. She knew Elvis, and even so, she was just as powerless as I was. Her words very carefully told me the truth. In the midst of the cruel message she sent, I sensed a warmth and compassion I had not anticipated. My image of a shallow woman disintegrated. The person who had written to me was different. Her kindness was not superficial but sincere. I felt that she meant every word she had written.

I was grateful. She had taken the time to reply. She had gone to great lengths trying to make our disappointment as mild as possible. She had not laughed at Karen's dream, but promised to help to the extent of her abilities. I wanted to thank her. I decided that I would write to her again.

As it turned out, I never got a chance to write and thank the Hollywood correspondent before we heard from her again. Two days later, the mailman importantly handed Karen a postcard, depicting the famous intersection at Hollywood and Vine. It read:

Dear Karen,
Miracle of all miracles! I called today and spoke to
Elvis himself on the phone. I told him all about you
and he was enormously touched to know that you love
him so much. He said he would like to send you something, and I gave him your address.

Love,
Marianne

Karen looked stunned. Her face turned a sickly white
and for a moment I thought she was going to faint. Her
mouth opened and closed convulsively as if she were trying
to speak, but not a word came across her lips. Her eyes hurried between the postcard and my face, and then back
again. I felt a quivering nausea in my stomach and knew
that in a few minutes I was going to be violently sick.

Hours seemed to go by while we remained frozen in
motionless shock. I was just as surprised as Karen. I was at
a complete loss to understand what had happened. Just as I
had finally come to grips with the idea that we would never
reach Elvis, just as I had at last fully realized that Karen
would never see her dream fulfilled, then suddenly this!
Only a couple of nights ago, I had cried out in pain over
the Hollywood correspondent's apologetic letter. She had
admonished me not to expect anything from Elvis and I
had dutifully obeyed her instructions. What had happened? How? Why?

I finally got enough control over myself to wheel the
stupefied Karen down to the bedroom. I helped her carefully onto the bed and sat down beside her to read the postcard once again. Through some infinite miracle, the words
were still there and the message was still the same. The
Hollywood correspondent had spoken to Elvis personally.

How in the world had she done it, I wondered. Was it sheer luck or was she really better acquainted with him than she had led me to believe? She said that she had told him about Karen and that he was touched. The enormous implication of that sentence overwhelmed me. It was no longer a one-sided relationship. Now he knew about Karen. He knew that she existed somewhere. He knew of her love. He cared. He cared. . . .

Karen lay absolutely motionless on the bed, except for an uncontrollable twitching of her hands. Her eyes were full of tears. Disbelieving, frightened tears.

"Karen," I said with a voice too thick and too hoarse to be mine. "He cares! He cares!"

And then suddenly I felt the tears streaming down my own face, as well. I embraced Karen and together we cried. We cried with all the emotion, all the frustration, all the horrible, doubting fear that had been building up within us for so long. We reached for each other in relief and desperation and allowed all our imprisoned feelings to pour out of our hearts along with the tears. I read the postcard over and over again to Karen, until we both knew it by heart.

When we were finally all cried out, we washed our faces and sat together on the bed. I had my arm around Karen who held the postcard in her hand with the same trembling carefulness you would hold a priceless jewel, turning it over and over again to examine every angle, every detail. She was still too astounded to fully realize what it meant.

With just the slightest feeling of doubt over my frequent doubts in the past, I sent a silent, thankful prayer to the Almighty who had indeed heard my prayers and performed a miracle for Karen.

It was not until much later that afternoon that Karen suddenly looked at me in bewilderment and asked, "But who, exactly, is Marianne?"

During the next few days, Karen and I went through several manic-depressive stages. One minute we would sit quietly, side by side in the playroom, sharing the same inscrutable, mysterious smile. The next moment we would be beset by a panicky urge to run to Karen's bedroom and worriedly reassure ourselves that the postcard was still there, carefully hidden in her nightstand. The glances we shared were triumphant. There was a sense of unreality about the situation, so intense and at times so threatening that neither one of us would have been surprised to suddenly wake up and find that it was all just a wonderful dream. But we did not wake up, and the postcard was always exactly where we had left it, carrying the same sacred message.

The compassionate Hollywood correspondent had kept her promise. She had cared enough about a little girl, whom she had heard about only in a letter, to use her influence and make that crucial contact directly with Elvis. Karen was no longer just an anonymous member of that roaring crowd of fans at his feet. Now he knew of her. Apparently, the Hollywood correspondent had told him enough about Karen to evoke some sort of emotional response. "Enormously touched," she had called it.

I thought about the way she had described Elvis in her letter. Polite. Well mannered. Shy. Somehow, those were not words I had expected to hear used in connection with a man in his position and with his fame. Confused, I saw all my prefabricated ideas and convenient labels of both Elvis and the Hollywood correspondent fall away, revealing two compassionate, caring human beings.

Was it possible that I was not the only one to see the tragedy in Karen's situation? Could it be that her story meant something to Elvis?

The final test still remained, of course. Would he actually send Karen something, or would he forget about her?

Karen's thoughts traveled the same emotional roller coaster. Her expression was confident and jubilant one minute, and full of worry the next. She was only one uncertain step away from the fulfillment of her dream. She stood at the threshold of happiness. Elvis knew of her.

How would he respond?

Karen vacillated between exhilaration and agony. For the next few days we made it a habit to wait by the window each morning until the mailman had made his delivery. Winter drew its first chilly breath when our waiting reached its end. A handful of lonely snowflakes fell gingerly through the air, letting us know that Christmas was only weeks away.

The headmistress was already by the table in the hallway, sorting through the mail. She gave me a strange look as she flipped through the pile in her hand and pulled out a thin envelope. With a twinge of guilt, I remembered that I owed her some sort of explanation. But the headmistress was much too wise a woman to ask any questions, and just smiled tenderly at Karen.

"Here is something for you, my dear." she said.

Breathlessly, Karen accepted the letter. Only a glance was necessary for her to realize that what she held in her hand was the fulfillment of her dream. There on the for-eign-looking envelope was her name in the unmistakable handwriting of Elvis Presley. By this time, we had both seen his autograph so many times. There was no question about it.

All at once, as if the machinery of time had suddenly broken down, there was silence and stillness. For what must have been several minutes, we all froze in our positions, like images on a screen when the projector is suddenly stopped: Karen, staring motionless at the letter in her hand; myself, with the frightening feeling that this was not real, it could not possibly be happening; the headmistress, halfway through her mail, who must have sensed the im-portance of the moment, that something awesome was tak-ing place in front of her eyes.

Karen's eyes were glued to the letter, almost as if she were afraid it might disappear if she allowed her gaze to waver. I saw a faint tremor work its way from her neck down her back. The headmistress regarded her intently. Somewhere from above us came the muffled sounds of laughter and crutches pounding against the floor, so distant and so unreal as if we were listening to the sounds from an-other world. I did not dare move for fear of breaking the magic spell that seemed to have embraced us.

Another trembling went through Karen's body. Her knuckles turned white and her fingers became rigid around the envelope. Then still another quivering tremor shook her, this time with brutal power. ◉

Instantly, the spell was broken. The headmistress's mail scattered all over the floor as we both came to Karen's rescue. Suddenly some evil force was shaking her brittle little body relentlessly. It took both of us to keep her in her wheelchair. Her seizure seemed to be without end. Her torture continued while the worried expression on the headmistress's face grew more and more serious. Terror choked my throat. I could not speak.

"Dear God," I thought desperately. "This is going to kill her. She will die right here in my arms and she won't even get a chance to read the letter."

It took at least ten minutes of agony before the convulsions finally subsided to the point where the headmistress was able to break away. She fled into her office and returned seconds later with a syringe which she callously thrust into Karen's arm. After one or two last, heaving spasms, the seizure ended and Karen fell back in her chair, completely limp. Her eyes were closed and her hair was moist with perspiration.

Quickly, efficiently, the headmistress wheeled her down to her bedroom and lifted her onto the bed. Karen's face looked ashen and drawn. Her limbs were shivering slightly, as if she were very cold. It was a natural reaction after the violent seizure she had just been through. In the past ten minutes, her body had been subjected to more stress and strain than a heavy laborer is in a day.

I was frightened beyond words.

"Is she going to be all right?" I whispered, unable to hide the fear in my voice.

"I don't know. She is exhausted."

The headmistress turned and looked at me, and I noticed that she too looked frightened. Her usual efficient composure was gone, and the tender smile which I thought was an integral and eternal part of her features was no longer there. She looked worried and tired.

"What's in the letter?" she asked tersely.

I should have known that the question would be coming, but I had not had a chance to prepare myself. Somehow, I had counted on a little more time.

Karen stirred in the bed.

"The letter!" she whimpered. "Where is my letter?"

The headmistress placed it gently in her hands. A shimmering smile fluttered across Karen's face as she clasped it between her fingers.

"I told you," she murmured to herself. "I told you he would write—"

Perhaps the headmistress took her cue from the serene expression on Karen's face because her look seemed softer as she turned to me again.

"It's a dream," I said. "A miracle."

She regarded me thoughtfully.

"It's a long story. I think Karen should be the one to tell you," I added self-consciously.

"It's from a friend of mine," Karen whispered from the bed. "He is really my friend."

The headmistress let it go at that. After instructing me to let Karen rest for the remainder of the day, and after repeated warnings to stay close to her every minute, she gave Karen a careful embrace and said, "You know, I am so very, very happy that you got a letter from your friend. From now on, I will pay extra careful attention to the mail to see if there is anything for you."

As she left the room with a soft rustle, I noticed that her usual gentle smile had returned to her lips.

Of all the people that have passed though my life, only a handful have left an impressive mark on my memory. One or two for their friendship and loyalty. Some for their intelligence. A few others for their skills and accomplishments. But there is only one that truly deserves to be called "great." There is a special corner in my heart where Elvis stands out for his kindness and generosity. He proved to be even more humane and caring than I had ever thought possible. I was astounded to discover that behind the image of the glamorous movie star there was a compassionate, sincere human being. Karen was, of course, not at all surprised. Somehow, she had known his true nature all along, and his letter only reinforced her conviction.

That afternoon in Karen's room, I made my first acquaintance with Elvis's true personality and I too became his friend.

Karen lay on her bed, savoring the miraculous happiness that suddenly was hers. The aftereffects of the violent seizure, along with the sedatives and muscle relaxants the headmistress had given her, had made her sluggish and drowsy, and she had a hard time keeping her eyes open. But the smile on her lips was confident, and the expression on her face serene. Her most sacred dream had come true and there was nothing left to wish for. Suddenly, the girl that nobody wanted had ceased to exist. She had been transformed into a royal princess. She looked as if she owned the most precious treasure in the world. And when I thought about it, I realized that indeed she did.

Since Elvis spoke a language different from ours, I was assigned the role of translator. With a mere glance out of her sleepy eyes, Karen commanded me to read the letter over and over until each word was inscribed in her heart.

It was not a long letter. The words were scribbled hastily and somewhat carelessly, and, indeed Elvis mentioned that he was in a hurry. But the tone of the letter more than compensated for its brevity. It was the kind of letter you write to a dear, old, valued friend, letting him know that your life is hectic, but not so hectic that you cannot take the time to let him know that you are thinking about him. Elvis said that he had learned of Karen's efforts to reach him and he was truly sorry that he had not responded sooner. His mail was so enormous and his time so scarce that he simply was not able to read it all. However, he wanted very much to be Karen's friend. He would like to hear more about her, about her life and friends and interests, so that he could really get to know her. To that end, he gave her a special address where letters would be sure to reach him. He invited her to write again, and promised that next time his reply would be longer.

That was the extent of it. But that was all that was needed. He had stepped out from behind the facade of the glamorous movie star and showed himself to be a very real, compassionate human being who truly cared that a little girl loved him. It mattered to him. It was important. He needed her, and he was aware of it.

He did not have to give her an address to write to, I thought. The fact of the letter itself would have been enough. He did not have to promise still another letter. He could have thanked her, or simply written his autograph on a piece of paper and stuck it in an envelope. Nothing beyond that was really necessary. Karen's dream would still have been fulfilled.

What a beautiful, generous person!

Karen was smug, complacent.

"I told you!" she kept repeating. "I told you all the time."

Yes, indeed. She had told me. I thought back over the past seven months and the innumerable times she had reassured me that there was no need to worry. Elvis would answer her letters. He would become her friend. How had she known it, I wondered. How had she been so sure? But, of course, I already knew the answer. Faith alone had provided her with a miracle. She had believed so strongly, so invincibly, that she would reach Elvis that there was no other way. It had to happen.

And it had happened.

With a voice so sleepy and so weak that it was barely audible, Karen begged me to read the letter again. I could tell that she was on the verge of giving in to her body's demands for rest. Dutifully, I read Elvis's letter one more time. By the time I reached the end, Karen had succumbed to her enormous fatigue and was sound asleep. The smile on her lips was still there. Jubilant. Victorious. Contented. Karen's life had turned in a new direction. Gone was the misery, the loneliness and the pain. Elvis had arrived. The prince with the mournful eyes and the velvety voice had claimed his princess. Was she dreaming now that they were riding off into the sunset?

Careful not to disturb her, I tucked the letter firmly between Karen's fingers. I wanted it to be right there when she woke up. I felt a sudden need to thank somebody, but was not sure who deserved my gratitude the most—the good Lord or Elvis Presley.

Exhausted, I sat back to examine the peaceful face of the little girl that I loved so dearly. She had brought me so much pain, such endless worry. She had taught me the difficult lesson of helplessness and despair. Now she had also shown me the importance of faith, and the fact that miracles do happen. Not one dream had been fulfilled that day, but two. Karen had found Elvis and my prayers for a morsel of happiness for this suffering, lonely child had been answered.

Two twentieth-century miracles.

Karen woke up the following morning with a healthy glow in her face and enthusiastic determination written in her eyes. From that moment on, her speech started improving, her muscles became more obedient, and her movements were remarkably manageable. Suddenly she was relaxed, open, harmonious. Happiness creates wonders that are far-reaching and inspiring.

More than once I saw the headmistress observing Karen from a distance, shaking her head in amazement and disbelief. I made myself a silent promise that someday I would tell her the whole story about Elvis so that she could understand the miracle she had witnessed.

Almost overnight, winter overtook the countryside. Christmas was near. In the middle of the noisy anticipation and feverish preparation for the holiday season, Karen and I sat down to write a letter to Elvis.

By now, the scene was old and familiar. Still, it was the first time ever. This time Elvis had *asked* Karen to write. Her letter would not make its journey blindfolded, in dreadful uncertainty of its final destination.

Karen was awed by the idea that Elvis was waiting, that his fingers would be touching the same sheet of paper she was touching, and that his eyes would be scanning each word she produced. Since this was such a special occasion, demanding every effort to get all the little details just right,

I had bought Karen a box of flowery, romantic notepaper. It was sheer and feminine, fit for a princess writing to her prince.

As always when we needed privacy, we had sought refuge in the deserted bedroom. There in the stillness of the late afternoon, with only faint and distant reminders of the frenzy that existed in the rest of the Brown House, we escaped the Christmas preparations in order to take care of a more important matter.

Karen used all her willpower to keep her muscles under control so that the letters would be neatly and evenly formed. She thought carefully and for a long time about each sentence. Every word, every phrase was critically scrutinized before it was judged, and nothing less than perfect was accepted. She bit her lip. She frowned in comtemplation. Occasionally, she asked my advice. Touched, I discovered that a love letter from a little girl to a great man is not at all different from any other love letter.

Once again, I had been assigned the job of translator. I felt proud and privileged to have this important function. Each time Karen gave final approval to another sentence, she quickly demanded that I translate it into Elvis's own language, spelling it out slowly for her to copy. She strained. She labored. But the little smile that seemed to have become a permanent part of her features these days never left her face, and I knew that no effort would have been too difficult for her when it came to Elvis. I smiled too. I felt a gratitude so vast that it approached reverence for the Almighty and for Elvis. And I also thanked them for the privilege of being a witness to it all.

The first evening shadows fell over the treetops when the letter finally was finished. Against regulations we sneaked out for a quick trip to the mailbox. Considering the importance of our errand, we felt justified in breaking the rules for once. The air felt clean and crisp, and a light snowfall sent a gentle cascade of white, twinkling little stars over the world. The Brown House stood among the trees, its lighted windows offering comfort to any weary traveler.

When we returned to the playroom, we found to our delightful surprise that it had been dressed in holiday colors with silver bells, gingerbread men, and fragrant pine wreaths hanging everywhere. The children were busy making and wrapping gifts for friends and relatives. The headmistress had even allowed a sparkling fire in the huge stone fireplace. Karen smiled tenderly and reached out to squeeze my hand in secret understanding.

It was going to be a good Christmas.

A day or two later, the mailman brought Karen a Christmas present. The box was big and beautiful.

With trembling hands, Karen unwrapped her gift. The layers of brightly colored holiday paper fell aside and revealed the biggest, brownest, cuddliest teddy bear ever. Stuck to his soft, furry tummy was a scribbled note that read:

My name is Teddy, and I have come a long way to wish you a very merry Christmas!

—Elvis Presley

Dear Elvis,

Thank you so very much for the teddy bear that you sent me. He is beautiful. He sits on my bed, and every time I look at him I think about you. I never had my own teddy bear before, and since you gave him to me, he is very special. Thank you again.

Most of all, thank you for being my friend. I always knew we would be friends someday. I really did write you several letters. I knew something was wrong when you did not answer. Now, I am so happy that we can write to each other. It means so much to me. I like you very much. I know everything about you already. You asked me to tell you something about myself. I am almost nine and I live in a boarding school because I have cerebral palsy. I cannot walk, so I have to use a wheelchair. I exercise every day. I don't think I am too pretty, but I hope that won't make any difference. Perhaps we could be friends, anyway? I think that you are so handsome and so kind and I am really very happy that you did write. Thank you again.

Love,
Karen

Dear Karen,

This is written in a big hurry, because I don't have much time but I wanted to thank you for your letter. I feel that I know you better already and I sure want to be your friend. Pretty has nothing to do with it. Believe me, I see pretty ladies all the time and it gets to be a bore. Being real is what counts, and I can tell that you are. I'm on my way to Nashville to cut a record. If it turns out okay, perhaps I will send you one. In the meantime, I hope you will write again so that I have a letter from you by the time I return to L.A. Take care of Teddy.

Love,
Elvis Presley

That Christmas was delightful and lovely. For the first time in her life, Karen was an excited participant in caroling, cookie baking, and gift giving. If there was any last remnant of the invisible wall, behind which she had hidden for so many years, it came down during those holiday weeks. Like a butterfly carefully emerging from its cocoon, she revealed a generous and affectionate, although still very shy, personality. The lines in her face softened. The hostile frown which for so long had served to keep everybody at a distance was replaced by an inviting, playful little smile. Her appetite improved, and she even added a few pounds to her skinny frame.

The children in the Brown House reacted as if they had suddenly been introduced to a new friend. The staff physician devoted page after page to Karen in his weekly reviews. The headmistress kept sending me glances which were both bewildered and grateful. I did not volunteer any explanations. Whatever clues I might have to offer were too personal in nature, and would have meant breaching the confidence Karen had placed in me. Besides, I was not all that sure that the medical profession would have understood the far-reaching effects happiness can have, and the importance of Elvis's presence in a little girl's life.

Christmas went by, but somehow the holiday magic lingered on. The next few months brought with them a winter more furious than we had seen in a long time. Man-high drifts of white, woolly snow reached the windows of the Brown House. The wind howled through the forest with ice-cold ferocity. We were snug and comfortable in front of the fireplace in the playroom, listening to music or talking about Elvis. The storm outside could not reach us.

We were safe and protected from any evil or distress the outside world might want to bring us. Elvis had seen to that. He had brought summer breezes and butterflies into our lives. He had given both of us a magnificent measure of happiness—Karen, by fulfilling her dream, and me, by allowing it all to happen right in front of my eyes.

As the weeks went by, his letters kept on coming. They were not frequent, and they were always hastily scribbled, but they kept on coming. That was all that really mattered anyway. Karen was the first to explain and excuse him for his busy schedule. She even went so far in her generosity and concern as to admonish him not to write at all, if it involved too much trouble. Fortunately, Elvis did not listen. It did not take long before a regular pattern of correspondence had developed. Every now and then, unexpected packages and presents were delivered. Records, photographs, T-shirts—always with the same, lovely message: "To my friend Karen, from Elvis Presley."

Dear Elvis,

Thank you for the letter and pictures. I was so surprised. I especially liked the one with the monkey. He looked so funny. I understand how busy you are. If you are too busy, you don't have to write. But if you have a moment, it would be nice to hear from you. It doesn't matter if it is short. I understand. I really do. I would like to send you a present too, but it is hard for me to get to a store.

I am listening to one of your records while I am writing this and I am so proud to know you. I haven't told anybody that I know you. I like to have your friendship for my very own secret. I hope you don't mind. How did it go in Nashville? I just know you did a great job as usual. You always do. So far, you haven't made any records that I didn't like. I even saw you in a movie once. That's when I knew we would be friends, and look what happened! If you are too tired when you come back home, don't even bother to write. I love you anyway.

Karen

My friend, Karen:

I was pleased to return to L.A. and find not only one but two letters from you. You said you are happy to be my friend. Well, let me tell you something. It is just as important to me to have you for my friend and I am very proud to know you. You sound like some outstanding little girl! It is OK with me if we keep it a secret. It's really nobody else's business but yours and mine anyway, right?

Nashville was hectic and I'm exhausted but it was good being back home for a while. I had a nice visit with my family in Memphis. I'm glad you liked Scatter. He is a chimp—lots of fun and lots of trouble! Will tell you more about him later. Right now, I'm going to eat something and go to bed. Hope you understand.

Write soon,

Elvis Presley

To my friend, Elvis:

How are you? It has been a while since I heard from you and I hope you are not sick, only busy. I am doing fine. I have been thinking a lot about what I could send you, but I guess you have everything already. Is there anything special you would like? I have drawn some pictures for you. They are not too good, I'm afraid, but I'm sending them anyway. My hands are stiff and shaky and it is hard for me to do a really good job. I did the best I could because I wanted to give you something. You have given me so much! I am so grateful for all the presents and I love you very much, if that means anything. I hope it does. Have you cut any more records? I got the ones you sent me and they were wonderful! You cannot buy those records here yet, so it is really something special! If you have a minute, please let me know that you are well and that we are still friends.

All my love,

Karen

God Bless You. Thanks.

Elvis

Dear Elvis:

Thank you for your short note. I know now that you are busy. I don't mind, just as long as we are still friends. I wonder if you are making more records or if you are doing a picture? There is not much happening here. I always have a lot of time. Sometimes we go for walks, and I like that very much. Do you? I also spend a lot of time listening to your music and looking at your presents. I wish I could come and visit you someday. Perhaps you could come here? That would really surprise everybody!

I am sending you a picture of myself so you will know what I look like. Do you think I should cut my hair? If you think so, then I will do it.

It is getting late and I have to go to bed now. I will write to you again tomorrow. Remember that I will always be your friend and I love you very much.

Karen

My friend Karen,

Thanks for letters and pictures. And I thought you said you were not pretty!!! I'm so glad you like my records. Music is very important in a lot of ways, you know. If you are happy or sad, it always seems to help. No matter what language you speak, you can always understand music. I think you know what I mean. I just finished playing football with Scatter and some of my friends. You can imagine how that game went! I'm starting a movie and expect to be pretty busy. Don't worry too much if you don't hear from me for a while. Don't cut your hair! I like it just the way it is. Keep writing, though! We will still be friends.

Elvis

P.S. I love you, too.

It is fascinating to explore any new friendship, only perhaps slightly more so when your friend is a world-famous entertainer. Little by little, we discovered the man behind the star. He was honest and unsophisticated, with a taste for the simple and down-to-earth ingredients in life: good friends, home cooking, and music. Although he appreciated the good fortune that had come his way, he also seemed overwhelmed by it. Confused. Perhaps even surprised. The innocent country boy with his close family ties, deep religious feelings, and good sense of humor was still there, despite Hollywood's efforts to turn him into a sex symbol and a money machine. The tone of his letters was unmistakably sincere. Why did he keep writing? There was nothing to gain. His correspondence with Karen was personal and secret, without even so much as an ounce of publicity attached to it. The answer was simple: he cared.

In spite of his stardom, and in spite of his wealth, he still had not lost touch with reality. Despite the labels of "superstar" and "overnight success" that the record and movie industry were pasting all over him, he was still a human being with feelings, emotions, and needs. He remembered how it felt to be poor and struggling. He knew what it meant to fight for survival and to endure each new day that rose above the horizon. He had lived through it himself, and it had put a mark on his soul that he could not easily forget. Now he was reaching out, in compassion and love, to a child in a similar situation. He was pouring sunshine and joy into her life with unselfish generosity. It was remarkable. It was unbelievable. It was beautiful.

I wondered where, exactly, Karen fit in and what function she fulfilled in Elvis's life. I sensed that she was important to him, not as a fan, but as a friend and a human being, someone who liked him for himself, the man behind the public image.

"My friend, Karen"—that was how he referred to her, time and again, in his letters. It was almost as if he wanted to remind himself that somewhere out there, among his millions of fans, there was one who asked that he accept her friendship. I had always heard that life at the top was lonely. Now I learned exactly how miserable and lonely it really was.

Karen blossomed. With each passing day, with each new letter from Elvis, she became softer, warmer, even more feminine. During the winter she slowly changed from an ugly duckling into a beautiful swan. By early spring of the following year, the frightened, hostile, suffering child was gone. She had grown into an open, harmonious, almost pretty young lady. Her face was relaxed. Her limbs were relatively obedient. There were moments when her movements were almost graceful. Like any other young girl, love had performed its miracle.

For each letter she received from Elvis, Karen sent him four. There was so much to tell, so much to ask. She had to make up for all those lonely years when Elvis was nothing but a dream in her heart. Not a day passed without a sentence or paragraph being composed. Whenever a letter was finished, Karen started a new one.

It was a rich, satisfying, glorious time. Karen was on top of the world. Pain, suffering, and loneliness were nothing but evil memories from out of the past. Happiness moved into our lives and made itself comfortable. It settled down as if for a long stay.

And while Karen was jubilantly savoring every drop and every morsel of her newfound bliss, winter gradually retreated and made way for a soggy, unfriendly spring.

A miracle had taken place. A dream had been fulfilled.

We all have dreams. Secret, unrealistic, comforting

dreams about what we would like to be, to have, to do. Dreams that momentarily take the gloom and drudgery out of our lives when things are just too much to bear. In this present age of fear and violence, perhaps our dreams are especially important, or even necessary, for survival. For some more so than for others.

Certainly, our need for dreams must also be the ultimate reason that movie stars and rock performers have such enormous importance in so many lives. Thousands of common, everyday people carry around the secret hope of someday, somehow, meeting their idol. I would venture to say that we create idols because we need them. They fulfill an important function in millions of lives. And because superstars are only human beings, too, with real feelings and emotions, the possibility is always there that a dream may come true. It did for Karen.

In late April, spring brought drizzling mornings and soggy afternoons. The sky looked like a soiled rag hanging above the tree-tops and the Brown House stood naked and uncomfortable in the chilly showers from above.

Spring colds and the flu made their rounds among the children and the headmistress mercilessly ordered even the slightest runny nose to bed. Karen was one of them.

For a couple of days she fought with a stubborn temperature that would not go away despite medication. She seemed to be in the grip of a virulent flu. Propped up in bed, two big, red roses on her cheeks and a feverish glow in her eyes, she was writing joyously to Elvis. All of his letters were scattered across the blanket. Photographs and pictures were strewn everywhere. From a corner, Teddy surveyed the disorder with his brown, glassy eyes.

Karen was hard at work printing row after row of crooked little letters. Her fingers were cramped and rigid around the pen, and her hair fell carelessly over her flushed cheeks. The tenderness in my heart was so overpowering that I could not help a smile.

"How do you spell—" Karen began, but interrupted herself in mid-sentence. "What are you smiling at?"

"At you."

"Why?"

"Because I love you."

She grinned and leaned back against the pillows.

"I know," she said with a little sigh of satisfaction.

"And do you know something else?"

"What?" she wondered.

"Elvis loves you, too."

Her smile was too gentle, too sheer, too feminine to belong to just a little girl. It was the smile of a young woman very much in love.

"You love him, don't you?"

She nodded quietly. She turned and looked at the raindrops streaking against the window. For a moment, we both remained silent, each of us a captive of our thoughts.

It all seemed so strange, so unreal. Thinking back over my attempts to reach Karen, and the long dismal road in search of Elvis, I suddenly felt as if I were a player in a prearranged and predetermined game. Only six months earlier, I never would have believed that we would ever get through to Elvis. A year or so before that, you could not have convinced me that Karen would ever want me for her friend. Still, here we were, together. I did not understand how it happened, but Karen was happy at last and Elvis was very real.

"Karen, how did all this happen?" I asked.

"What?"

"You and me, Elvis, everything?"

"It just happened," she said simply.

"It seems so strange to think about it. I never would have believed."

"That was always your problem," Karen interrupted.

"What do you mean?"

"You never really believed it would happen."

"That's true. I didn't. But you, on the other hand—"

"I knew it all along," Karen said matter-of-factly. "I tried to tell you. I don't know why you wouldn't listen."

"But how did you know?"

"I just knew."

That was all there was to it. She resumed working on her letter, and I curled up at the foot of the bed to look at the sullen rain outside.

The afternoon was gloomy and it did not take long before Karen put down her pen and yawned drowsily. With half-closed eyelids and a happy smile she made herself comfortable among the pillows. Within minutes she was sound asleep. The weather was conducive to sleeping, and I looked at her with envy for a moment before I too allowed my eyes to close.

The Brown House enclosed us with its love and acceptance, a safe haven in a cruel and stormy world. It was our home, the only real home we both had ever known. The rain played a quiet, tapping tune on the window. Karen's breathing was soft and rhythmic. For an instant I thought about Elvis and the miraculous way in which he had changed our lives. Then I succumbed to the cozy feeling of peace and contentment that pervaded my soul, and drifted off into a confused, but lovely, dream about Karen running through a meadow of flowers, throwing letter after letter up into the blue summer sky. Each letter turned into a beautiful butterfly that flew on sheer, trembling wings toward Elvis who was waiting, smiling, at a distance.

I did not wake up until well into the night. The darkness was black and impenetrable, and silence was endless around us. The Brown House was sound asleep.

I groped awkwardly for the lamp on the nightstand and turned on the light. Everything was exactly the way we had left it. The bed was covered with Elvis's gifts and letters, and Karen was resting right in the middle of it with a peaceful, serene smile on her lips and her own letter to Elvis clasped tightly in her hand.

Still in the confused bewilderment of having overslept, I gathered up the letters and straightened out the disarrayed blanket. As I leaned over to give Karen a gentle kiss, I was overcome by an eerie feeling that something was terribly wrong. There was something missing, something vitally important that was supposed to be there but was not.

I looked at Karen. She appeared to be warm and comfortable. Her eyes were closed and the smile on her face was one of loving tenderness. She must be dreaming about Elvis. I thought to myself.

Just to be sure, I put my cheek against her forehead to check her temperature, but she was not feverish. On the contrary, she felt strangely cool. All at once, I realized what was wrong. The quiet, regular breathing had stopped. Her body was completely still under the blanket.

"Karen," I whispered in shock and disbelief. "Karen, wake up. Please, wake up!"

But she did not respond and when I tried to shake her limp, lifeless body there was no longer any doubt.

I felt a numbness spread through my limbs. It froze and deadened everything in its way. The pain and sadness I should have been feeling was locked in the stifling grip of shock. Not until hours later did the first tear roll down my cheek.

I stared at her face, so peaceful, so completely happy. Her smile was gentle and serene. The girl that nobody wanted had come a long way. The good Lord had been with us. He had given us the miracle of Elvis Presley. Now he had shown the infinite measure of his goodness and wisdom. He had taken Karen to the highest peak of happiness. He had allowed her the fulfillment of her dream, and had taken her away before any letdown or disappointment.

My legs were trembling and I knelt on the floor beside her. I did not cry—not then. There was nothing but emptiness within me as I held her thin body in my arms for the very last time. I talked to her—quiet, tender words of reassurance and love. I thanked her for our time together, and for the lessons she had taught me. I told her of the pain and loneliness that was waiting for me. I explained the bitter void she was leaving behind, not only in my life, but also in Elvis's.

In the silence of the night I lay there, whispering to Karen, saying goodbye. When the first morning light fell through the window, I finally got up and gave her one last farewell kiss on the forehead. Carefully, I pried loose the letter, clasped tightly between her fingers.

As I walked out the door, a line of poetry flashed through my mind: "Life must go on. I forget just why."

I went to my room and packed my things.

The early morning was wet and misty as I walked across the lawn. At the end of the driveway, I stopped and looked at the Brown House behind me. I had not spoken to anyone. Not even the headmistress. I wanted to be alone with my grief.

Not until I was safely on my train did I look at the letter I had taken out of Karen's hand, and felt the first tear-drop on my face. There, in uneven, scraggly little letters, she had spelled out:

To Elvis, with love . . .

Epilogue

Two years after Karen's death, I still had not quite figured out how to continue my life without her.

It was shortly after midnight, and the tender, blue California night wrapped itself snugly around the city. The air was warm and fragrant with summer. Just a hint of breeze came in from the ocean, rustling lightly through the palm trees.

I was aimlessly roaming the quiet streets of West Los Angeles in my secondhand Volkswagen. The motor hummed monotonously under the hood. The car radio was playing softly. I was smoking cigarette after cigarette, trying to cope with the gnawing restlessness inside me. I had no particular destination. I was just driving around, up one street and down another, because I could not think of anything better to do with myself.

The initial shock of losing her was over, and now loneliness threatened to drown me. It was fiercer this time, and much more difficult to handle. I was an easy target. For weeks after her death, I incarcerated myself in my apartment in Stockholm, barely eating or sleeping, just staring vacantly into space. I walked around from room to room, looking at all the familiar things as if I saw them for the first time. The phone would ring distantly, but I never answered. I could not think of anybody I really cared to talk to. I remember making tea and toast, and discovering it hours later—untouched—at the dinner table. I was in a trance, overpowered with grief. I would cry for hours on end, until my face got red and swollen and totally unrecognizable. I would sit and brood endlessly, thinking about Karen, the apparent futility of her life and mine, and wondering what it all added up to. I kept the record player going, day and night. Elvis's voice followed me from room to room. I read his letters to Karen, again and again. It was my only way of holding on to what had been.

I wanted nothing more than to get on the train, go back to the Brown House, and miraculously discover that Karen still was there. But I knew she was dead, and a warning voice from deep inside told me never to set foot in there again. And I never did.

I had lost my only real friend in the world. My daughter, my sister, was gone. My loneliness was suffocating me. The pain was slowly driving me insane. I discovered everything that Karen had really meant to me. To die would have been a relief, a last pleasure in life.

I felt like a leper, an outcast. I wondered bitterly what contagious disease I carried that caused the most important people in my life to flee so abruptly from my side. I was utterly alone, without family, without friends.

As the weeks went by, the pain in my soul reached such enormous proportions that it could not possibly get any worse. It settled into a hard, twisted knot in my stomach. But my basic instinct for survival must have been strong. Somewhere along the line, I started eating again, sleeping an hour here and an hour there, and making plans for escape.

Perhaps, if I got away, if I started all over in a brand new environment, everything would be different? Los Angeles was as good a place as any. Elvis lived there. So did Marianne, the Hollywood correspondent. People said that the opportunities were limitless in southern California. The sun was always shining, and the people friendly and smiling. Besides, it was just about as far away from Sweden as one could possibly go. . . .

I was free to make a new life. I was young, intelligent, and fairly attractive. Intellectually, I realized that my life was waiting for me. But the scars of the past were too fresh in my soul, and the bruises of loneliness still tender and sore. Instead of rushing into the future with joyful anticipation, I went reluctantly. To me, the future was only a means of running away from the past. Not until years later would I learn that there are some things that life forces you to live with forever. I was already marked as a loner, a roamer, and a dreamer. And I knew I would never change.

When I told my mother of my plans to leave, she gave me a quick kiss on the forehead and stuck some money in my hand. If there were any last traces of hesitation in my mind about my decision to go, that gesture quickly erased them. Without regret, I left Sweden to start a new chapter in my life.

Southern California was everything they said it would be—and more. Each morning the sun shone in a sky more blue than the day before. The beaches were white and the ocean spread further than the eye could see. Los Angeles offered me a choice of life-styles, of friends, a chance for a new purpose in my life.

I was impressed, sometimes overwhelmed. Slowly hope started rising within me. Surely, in a city so full of adventure and activity, there would be no place for painful memories.

I took an apartment in Westwood and enrolled at UCLA. Soon I made friends, bought a car, and started to feel at home in my new environment.

On the surface, I was doing fine. Each morning, along with makeup and mascara, I put a carefully rehearsed smile on my face before I went out to meet the world. At parties, I was friendly and outgoing. At school, I pretended hard to be interested in the lectures.

But there were always those moments when I was alone and my memories forced themselves to be heard. I could not forget Karen. I still missed her. I realized that there would always be a secret corner of my soul where loneliness loomed dark and menacing. For the rest of my life I would be searching desperately for a love like the one we had for each other.

I started writing about her. I did not want to forget. The story about Karen was too rare and too beautiful to ever be forgotten. Late at night, while the rest of the world was asleep around me, I sat at the typewriter and relived our time together.

I grew restless, and found it hard to concentrate on my studies. When the opportunity came to work as a teacher's aide in a little school for cerebral palsied children, I quickly grabbed it. I started my new job full of anticipation, feverishly believing that perhaps I had once again found a meaningful place in life.

But although the work itself contained many similarities to work in the Brown House, it was still not quite the same. The children were just as pathetic, just as full of love, and they needed me just as much. But it was not the Brown House. And I never found another Karen. If anything, it only served as a bitter reminder of all that I once had but which was lost forever.

After work, I would go home to my typewriter and recreate the past. At night, I drive aimlessly for hours through the streets of Westwood.

One night I decided, as I often did, to make one final turn past Elvis's home on Perugia Way before going home. It was comforting to know that he was there. He had loved Karen too. The Hollywood correspondent was the one who informed him of her death, and his letters stopped coming. Something intuitive told me that Karen took a little bit out of his life, too, when she died.

The winding roads through Bel Air were dark and deserted. The houses and mansions were resting peacefully behind their locked iron gates. The breeze brought a clean smell of freshly cut grass from the golf course.

The noise from my Volkswagen engine seemed loud and lonesome in the stillness of the night. The lights were on in Elvis's house, and I wondered if he, too, was brooding in the night, perhaps thinking about Karen.

As I completed the circle and emerged once again on Bellagio Road, there were suddenly headlights behind me. There were two of them. I slowed down on the twists and turns of the narrow street, but the lights kept their distance behind me. Slightly irritated, I pulled up to the red stoplight at Sunset Boulevard. Within seconds, two motorcycles joined me.

I turned my head and looked at the dark figure by my side. There, within reach of my arm through the open car window, straddled across a large Harley-Davidson, and dressed in black from top to toe, was Elvis himself. Slowly, perhaps feeling my stare, he turned to look at me. There were the familiar features I had become so well acquainted with. There was the face that Karen and I both had loved. There was seriousness written about his lips. His hands fiddled restlessly on the handlebars. And deep in his eyes was sadness and pain.

"Hi," he said quietly. It was more a movement of his lips than anything else.

The world suddenly came to a standstill. Time ceased to exist. There was only the unbelievable magic of being face-to-face with Elvis.

I gasped.

"Elvis—" I said. But the enchanted moment was over. The red light had turned to green, and my voice drowned in the roar as the two motorcycles made a turn onto Sunset.

He was gone.

On August 16, 1977, I was relaxing in the backyard of my California home. Life was happy and good. After nine years of misery, I had finally found the strength to untangle myself from a marriage which had long been going in the wrong direction. I was free, and the challenge of the life that lay ahead of me was something I could hardly wait to attack.

Only a few months earlier, on the spur of the moment,

I had gathered up my old writings about Karen and sent it to a literary agent in New York for consideration. To my surprise, he had called me only a week before with the exciting news that he believed that he would be able to sell it for publication. At last, I would be able to tell Elvis the whole story about Karen. I owed him much more than gratitude. Perhaps I would be able to finally do something in return. There were rumors about his involvement with drugs, young girls, and drinking. I, like so many other of his fans, was angrily refusing to believe them.

I was going to show the world what Elvis was really like, what a good man he was. It was the least I could do for him.

The phone rang in the quiet afternoon, and I left my two little boys playing in the grass to answer it. My children were the only ones who had ever been able to somewhat lessen the pain of Karen's death.

It was my friend and employer, Gerry, who sounded strangely excited.

"Did you hear?" she said.

"Hear what?"

"About Elvis?"

"What about Elvis? Did he get married?" I asked cheerfully.

"He died."

"Oh, come on!" I said lightly. "Elvis can't be dead. I haven't told him about Karen yet!"

Elvis dead? It was a joke. It had to be. An insane, cruel joke. He was too young, too full of life to die. And I had not thanked him yet. . . .

"Turn on the television," Gerry said abruptly, and hung up.

Hours later, when the horrifying truth had at last penetrated my numb brain and I was a sobbing, helpless soul, Gerry called again.

"How are you doing?" she said.

"It is not true. It can't be. I won't have it—"

"Are you crying? Do you want me to come?"

"It is not true. It is not true. It is not true—"

"Look," Gerry said thoughtfully. "Do you know what my first thought was when I heard about it?"

"Oh, Elvis—"

"I thought, perhaps now, at last, Karen will get to meet him."